Beating The

Michael David Decosta

Table Of Contents

Dedication

This book is dedicated to my mother, Genevieve Nora Decosta and to my brother Anthony Steanislaus Decosta.

Also, thanks go to my darling wife Angie and to everyone who helped make this book possible.

Introduction

People tend to usually pen down autobiographies about themselves when writing a first-person account of their lives in their own voice and style. The writer likes to tell the reader about his or her experiences from start to finish chronologically, that is, up to the point of writing the book. Impactful and important lives of famous people tend to have that quality. There is a great emphasis on history and facts.

I have decided to think of this book as a memoir rather than an autobiography. It only covers parts of my life, where the order of events and chronology are not the most relevant of my themes. My earliest temptation also was an autobiography, but I understood later that I don't really have to be precise about chronology and touch on all aspects of my interesting life for it to be a good first-person account of my life. After all, I am no Malcolm X or Benjamin Franklin. So yes, I have decided to concentrate on those memories that are especially important or vivid to me. You are going to read about the parts of my life that I can still remember; I shall convey to you the taste, the feel, and the smell. In other words, rather than facts or history, the emotional experience and interiority are more important for me in this book.

I have learned about all of this over the course of writing this book. And do you know what else have I learned through writing? That first of all, memories don't start with or end with a 'What Happened?' In fact, I don't think memories end at all. They go on changing and playing a game of hide and seek with your mind. At various instances, across various moods, you will remember a different colour of a memory. Objectivity will be aversive to you. You will be the central character, and hence, will remember only what you want to remember.

But I have battled this. Or at least I can say that I have done my best. I have sat with my memories for long and spent time with them. I drank coffee with them and showered with them. Only when I have felt that I know the perfect way to etch those memories down have I done so. That way, I know I have respected my reader.

I have also learned about the boons and bane of writing along the course of this book. The way memories and experiences exist in some metaphysical realm; writing acts as an instrument to pull them out and materialize that metaphysical. Writing is like a digging tool extracting the oil: you need the right kind of drill, power and an expert behind the operation of the tool.

That perfection in writing only comes through practice. In that way, writing is a muscle. If you don't flex it, test it, stretch it, it will never grow. No sir. That's why I have written and rewritten what you are going to read in the chapters to come. Do I expect my book to be a bestseller after all the blood, sweat and tears I put? Not really. If it becomes that, that's well and good, but my intention is something else. I just want whatever I put out of my life out there to make me really happy. I want it to come out polished.

People worry about writing a lot, but the hardest lesson I have had to learn is that writing is really only half the battle. Editing is just as crucial. You are going to eventually have to bite the bullet and just do it. And like writing, the more you do it, the better you will get at it. It will also improve your writing. It's a win/win; you just have to do it, and I know I have done it. I have edited and re-edited this book to bring out the polished form.

All these endeavours have worked to both show me what I can do when I set my mind to it, and more importantly, reflect on my own life too. I have thought about what has happened to me and can confidently say that the experiences that I have written down have made me live them again.

In this age of saturation, you have to stand out with your stories. And if you are going to stand out, not only does your work have to be top-notch, but you are probably going to have to get creative. I think that we are no longer living in an era when just being really good was enough. There are more folks churning out books than ever today who are really good, but they barely get noticed. I believe I can and will stand out. Hence here is my book.

While you read me and my words from here on out, read me as a dealer in memories. I believe I have done them justice. Some of my memories are over fifty years old now and yet are preserved crystal clear. I won't lie, but sometimes the startling clarity of them makes me doubt their reality. It makes me question also whether all the people that have known me remember what I remember?

I do not think that much is possible. Especially because memories interact with emotions, and emotions are highly subjective entities. Everyone mixes them up in their own way. It is very similar to making a meal. No two people can make even a dish simple and fish and chips or spaghetti and have them taste exactly the same. The same goes for memories. No two people can narrate them the same way.

But as I have said to you, I have done my memories justice. And it is my hope that you are fulfilled with the narratives I present to you, dear reader.

Chapter 1: Georgetown, October 1967

It was a warm and sunny day reported in Georgetown, but only weather-wise. Genevieve, my mother, was taken into the Public Hospital this day since her water had broke. She was to give birth to her sixth child on this day. The catch? There was to be no celebrations, no balloons, no congratulation cards... and above all no family surrounding her.

Genevieve Nora Decosta had left one failed marriage with four daughters and four countries behind her with their father. The world for my mother was not the most favourable place.

To give a bit of a background of my mother, Genevieve was a pretty young white woman in a mostly black country. The demographics were clear to her. For her, finding work as a woman of the night was very easy. After all, out of six, she had two young babies to feed and a rent to pay.

She was a very proud and stubborn woman nonetheless. No matter the times that came, she faced them head-on, in a very determined manner, with self-reliance and grit. She would not ask any of her family for help, even though this was the time she had hit that rock bottom. It will not be wrong to say she was a rule-breaker, a sort of rebel. Her family had put down an array of rules and restrictions, and my mother went on to break every single one of them. If I could name one thing that Genevieve prioritised the most and could not compromise on, was her autonomy. She was more than willing, in fact, she was hell bent on living her life the way she chose. Nothing was going to cage her.

It was under a mother of this temperament that I was born, and under the conditions aforementioned. After two days of giving birth to me, Michael David Decosta, my mother left the hospital with only the clothes on her back, a paper bag which contained two terry nappies, pins and an address of a priest at the Sacred Heart Roman Catholic Church in the city. There was nothing and no one else by her. What about the other five children, you may be wondering? My mother had left the four year old son Anthony with a friend that she had only met months before. When she had collected Anthony, she returned to her one- bedroom box of a room which was on Murry Street. She resulted in locking him and I in the room with only cow and goats milk powder and water as nourishment.

It would usually go that Anthony would scream for his mother in her absence. Me, his younger brother would just lay there helpless. When she was at home, I would wait for mother to be done with Anthony so that she could tend to me. When I was about six months old, my mother had me baptized with the vicar making himself my godfather. Once again, like during my birth, there was to be no celebration, no cake, no fuss. My baptism was just another day in the lives of my family members. I do not narrate any of this as complains, or in a complaining tone. I am only reporting and recalling things as they were.

After getting me baptized, my mother continued to work at night, leaving us boys all alone. Given her rock bottom period still persisted, she had also started drinking. For nothing else but to numb the shame and pain and to escape the misery of her situation.

Anthony eventually turned six years old. As they say in child development psychology, this is the age that the child starts becoming more aware of emotions, his own and those of others. While theory says that the child at this age shows improved ability to manage emotional stability and relative independence from the parents, since the world starts becoming more open and accessible to him.

At this age, Anthony wanted to know where his mummy kept going at night. It took him a while to understand the reality of the situation, and he thought himself a curious plot. One night, after his mummy had left for work, he managed to break himself from the tiny room. Thing was, he wasn't alone. He took his baby brother, that is me, with him, out of the room and therefore the house. We both found ourselves out on the street in the middle of the night, all on our own.

Anything could have happened to us at that moment, enough to have given my mother a heart attack. Fortunately, it wasn't too long before we were picked up by the Police and taken to the station. Anthony could not answer the questions the officers posed at him, and I could barely speak. My mother got done with work and returned home to find the boys had vanished. Naturally, after the panic and all, she had to go to the Police Station to report us missing. When she reached the station, there we were. I don't know what interaction took place between her and the Police, but it was here that my mother realised things had to change. She decided that this way of life could not continue, and that she was in no fit state to raise her boys.

Her plan for us then was going to bring a drastic change in our lives, especially for me. She began looking for a suitable home for us, for someone else to adopt us and give us the undivided nurturing we needed.

She had met with a fish vendor by the name of Clarice Moore, who didn't have any children of her own. My mother asked Clarice if she would like to take the boys in until she got back on her feet. She laid down her case and presented how Clarice could benefit with having the presence of children. Clarice expressed that she would love to help, but that she could only take one of the boys in. The fishing lifestyle did not bring that much of money in either. So she took me in, as I was still only a baby. Clarice was delighted.

The newly-become mother took her bundle of joy home to meet her husband, but he instantly disapproved of the arrangement. The reasons probably had to do with money again, but Clarice told him she didn't need his help. "I would raise Michael on my own."

Clarice's husband just kissed his teeth at her, shrugged his shoulders and left her to it. I was too young to remember any of this.

Meanwhile, with the help of the vicar, Anthony was soon sent to an orphanage. That was the very last time that he saw his mother or me, his little brother.

Chapter 2: Life On Clarice's Farm

Clarice and her husband lived on a small farm on the coast. For Clarice's husband, main priorities included spending his time womanising and breeding all types of domesticated animals. Clarice was a full-time worker. That was the difference between the two.

For a child, the farm was a wonderland of a place to be growing up in, especially after the shift from the very urban mode of life. No sooner, Michael had grown to love all the animals around. He developed a sensitive place for them too. But that was all about to change.

Clarice was a self-employed fish monger in the historic Bourda Market, known for being constructed in the 19th century and being enclosed with iron railings. With time passing, the number of vendors have had also increasing in the Market, and being accommodated too. Bourda Market is situated in the centre of Georgetown, about ten miles from Liliendaal, the village where Clarice used to live.

My everyday routine back then included waking up at dawn, and then Clarice taking little old me to work with her every morning at five o'clock. Though not really unique from others, I remember her stall vividly. I recall that at one end of the stall, she had a small cardboard box which would double up as a playpen and a bed for me.

10

From what people tell me, I was a very attractive baby. And you can imagine what having an attractive baby could do for a business. I drew passersby in, and it would make for a boisterous and jolly time. It would help for Clarice's stall, and more so, folks would bring me toys, books and some would even give me money.

When I was old enough, Clarice sent me to pre-school, before graduating onto St Barnabas Primary School. Convenience had it that the school was next door to the Bourda Market. Study and work neighboured side by side.

Everywhere around the Market that I went, I made friends easily, both with children and adults. They all seemed to love me. I was the favourite kid in town, and note-worthily, this was my first exposure to the outside world and secondary socialisation. All was coming along pleasantly.

I was able to reason with grown men at the age of four, having had to deal with customers every day. No surprise then that I was getting street smart. Everyone would be amazed at how clever I was. Out of some of the most memorable comments, one given to me was, "Hey, have you been on this planet before?"

A lot has been written about children who grow up quick at a young age. Nowadays, the millennials are known to relatively grow up lazier, living their lives before their screens. Much is said about how they "don't know how to do anything," or are impractical when it comes to real-world matters. There may be times when it is true, and when comparisons such as these are fairly done with people of our age. But it is also said that these children are growing at their pace.

I don't know to what extent it is pleasurable or not so that children have to learn things at a younger age due to conditions they are put under. What I do know is that each person has their own life trajectory. Some are forced to take care of their children entirely, some cook early and even pay the bills at their place. It is conditions of destitution that bring about these circumstances, one way or another. We can argue all day long the pros and cons of this way of life.

In contrast, there are children who grow up 'at their age', because they don't have to face the brunt of circumstance. That is a relatively privileged lifestyle that brings pros and cons of its own too. They say that 'adult' responsibilities should not be placed on a child, for the pressure may be too much to take. But I can only speak for myself, and my experience tells me that my trials and struggles have been blessing in disguise for me.

As a young boy in Liliendaal, I used to collect old tyres and porcelain sinks. You may wonder why? I used them to plant exotic sweet-smelling flowers and shrubs, such as beautiful flame red Hibiscuses. This wasn't just a hobby. My early life exposure and sensitivity to animals attracted me to all sorts. And my target here was swarms of exquisite butterflies and hummingbirds who would be in search of the nectar.

There was a large fence that boxed off a piece of land at the side of where I planted my flowers. This was where Moore had his vegetable garden. Over here, he grew Pigeon peas, kidney beans, callaloo, cassava, okras, eddos and dasheens. Also growing in Moore's garden was a large dong tree that bore really tasty dongs. These really were irresistible green kiwi shaped fruits even if you were an adult, never mind a young child. In short, this was a no-go zone for me. Area 51, as far as I was concerned, and the point was well infused by Moore.

I had experienced a lot of things at such a tender age already. But this was the time I was to experience my first real beating, coming from Moore, of course.

You see, what happened one day was, I opened the gate to Moore's Garden and climbed the dong tree, knowing well this was the forbidden fruit. I may have been growing up mature, but I was a kid still, not just at heart but body too. I wanted to sneakily get at some of the tasty fruits up the tree. The thing is, I may have succeeded, but the mistake I made was forgetting to close the gate behind me.

13

How exactly did that put me at risk? You may be wondering that Moore may have seen the gate open and suspected foul play. Wrong. Leaving the gate open let in about forty sheep and goats, who made their way into the garden and enjoyed a massive feast of Moore's vegetables. I was too little to have been able to control them all myself, so I let my hands down in despair.

When Moore saw these sights, he lost his temper. He flew into a fit of rage and gave me a hitting that to this day I cannot forget. Not the most fun times.

From this point onwards, life at home was now changing very fast for me. I had been given a load of chores to do, and I could make no excuses against it. I was by this time seven years old, and my first job at the start of the day was to clean up all the mess that our fourteen dogs had made. At night, I was supposed to feed all the dogs and make sure that they were locked away finely.

The other jobs I carried out throughout the day was to milk the cows, collect the eggs, clean out the pig pens, all of this before going to school, which was ten miles away. So many of you out there would start off your day waking up for school as a child. Not me. By that time, it was as if the middle part of my day.

To reach the school, I had to catch the National Bus into the City, but sometimes would hitch a ride on a horse-drawn cart from another farmer going along. I decided this latter option was more fun since I additionally got to spend my bus fare on sweets. The child instinct again.

As far as school life was concerned, it worked out extremely well for me, thankfully. The best part was that I got to make a lot of friends. The second best part perhaps was that I could use my imagination to its fullest. Another fun part was that the school supported my love for sports. Who knew that I would be able to make it into the cricket team, football team and the rounder's team. Life all in all seemed to be going well since coming over to and living on Clarice's farm.

Though no one from home came to support me or attend events such as sports day, parent's evening or in fact anything else that had to do with school. When I say back at home, I am talking Liliendaal, of course, where lived Mr Moore and his wife Clarice, as you already know. But additionally, there also were first woman Lena and second woman Sue. Actually, you can also add Lewis, since Lena had given birth to him, a baby boy.

So, all of this meant that I had more and more jobs to do.

Chapter 3: The Killings

In this part of the world where I hailed from, we lived in what were called stilt houses. As the name explains it, these houses were built on stilts, or rather these were like normal houses that were raised on stilts. This was because of the country being below sea level. Stilt houses protected us from flooding, and kept the vermin away too. An indirect benefit of stilt houses is that the shady part underneath the flooring can be used as storage.

While our houses towered a little bit like that, the pigsty and cow pens were all built on ground level with a partition for every individual pen. That's just how everybody kept them. At any one, we would have up to twelve pigs in. The breeding sows were kept together.

As was the norm, all the male piglets were castrated at the age of six weeks, save for one pig from each batch. This one male would serve the breeding purposes to produce more piglets in the future. In case you are wondering why the pigs were castrated, there are various reasons. Castration prevents what is called the boar taint among the meat of male pigs when they reach puberty. Then, castration also helps prevent unwanted reproduction and reduces the aggressive behaviour of the pigs.

It was not an easy job to castrate the pigs. I would call it a gruesome process. I was given the job of holding the Piglets' legs while my foster father Moore chopped off the balls of the poor creature, dropping them into an old coffee tin. Following this, salt would be put onto the wound. This was repeated until all of the piglets were castrated. Let's just say one eventually becomes numb to it. And I am still glad that I wouldn't be the one doing the chopping.

Fridays would be our slaughter day. This was another thing that I would be made to watch but never took part in. Well, until I was nine years old.

After the age of nine, slaughtering and preparing the animals was now added to my list of things to do on the farm. Two people were required for the slaughtering process, because killing was a two-man job. It was done by having one person on the back of the pig while the other knelt on the front. Then a very sharp sword-like knife would be used. It was pushed into the throat, towards the breast area, penetrating the heart of the pig.

The pigs always made a racket when slaughtered. It was a horrifying sound. I haven't forgotten it to this day. After the slaughtering, the knife would be removed from the pig. A small bucket would be placed under the pig's body to collect all the blood. The blood needs to be drained from the pig to procure clean, edible meat.

After blood collection, I would then build a fire, putting a forty-five-gallon drum cut in half, and then would fill it with water, which would be left to boil. After the water would be boiled, the pig would be lowered into it for about three to four minutes. After this, the pig would be placed onto the worktop, where the scrapping would take place for the removal of the hair. That's what the boiling process is for, to soften up the hair on the pig's body. During the hair removal process, the pig would be put back into the water from time to time until all the hair would be removed. Then two holes would have to be made in the back legs so that the carcass could be hung up in preparation to have all of the insides removed, cleaned inside and out, and saved along with the blood. This was used to make black pudding.

The remains would be put together along with any fish that Clarice brought back from the Market into the boiling water and then used for food for the dogs. Nothing really got wasted in the process.

There was no fridge in the house, so customers who normally bought meat would come on the same day as the kill. Some meat would be saved for cooking and pickling.

Sometimes, while the dog food was cooking, I would place a couple of eggs into the water. When they were boiled, I'd eat them and wash them down with some coconut water. On Saturdays, if I didn't go to help out at the Market, my friend Jerry would pop round and we would have what they called Bush Cooked Rice and Peas. Again, we would wash this down with lots of coconut water. It is said to be very nutritious along with being delicious, of course!

It was only on Saturday that my foster father Moore would not be home. He would go to the Market to buy animal feed, so while the cat would be away, the mice would play! Jerry and I would join the other boys, Cranny, Ron and many others for a swim in the canal. We would dive to the bottom to catch Tilapia fish from one of the many tyres that the local fishermen would have planted at the bottom. These fish were relatively common round us. But the local fishermen, they were quite something. If we ever saw them while diving and catching fish, they would scream and shout. Oh, how we used to find that funny and enjoyed it to no limit.

The water supply was fed via a large pipe running over the canal. We boys would balance on the pipe and wrestle with each other. Why so? To grab the pipe! The last person standing with the pipe in hand would be crowned King of the land. That's interesting memory from childhood.

If I'd tell you the truth, I only really had two friends. Apart from Jerry and Cranny, I always felt alone. And as is psychologically natural, I started to want more companies, therefore tried so much to fit into society. This meant into school, with my family and friends. However, no matter how hard I tried, I didn't feel like I truly belonged anywhere. Funnily enough, I would think about how I just felt like a UFO sometimes (if they exist).

It's not like my family was like the family of my friends or of those around me. My household was so very different in so many ways, and even with them, I was an odd one out. We had our own different approach to doing things, our own way of thinking, our own way of walking, even our fashion sense did not really match.

I was unique appearance-wise too in the village. I had immensely soft and curly hair that would shine in the sun, while others' was coarse. My skin was like cocoa or light chocolate, while everyone else was really dark. So, I stood out, even if and when I did not want to.

Chapter 4: Facing Death

Over the years, I had learned that the most horrible and obnoxious thing imaginable about life was… the element of sudden change. What I mean is that life is so flimsy, and the wall between life and death, between extraordinary beauty and mind-boggling ugliness, can take only a second to turn it upside. It takes one moment for your head to hit the ground and feet be up in the air. One second your life appears idyllic, and the next it's gone. Life can become topsy-turvy like that. As a boy, I once read an aphorism that has stuck with me until today. It said, "Don't tell me that the sky is the limit when there are footprints on the moon." In that way, I always loved pushing my limits and not stopping at the boundaries set or accepted by others. Tell you what, it's a real joy to soar higher than everybody else around you.

Most people would tell you that death is the cruellest thing. I am not among those most people. I disagree with this notion too, just like with that 'sky is the limit' one. I would without hesitation tell you that death is not the cruellest thing, and it would not be a superficial statement. For I have seen so many of my friends die over the years. Heck, I have even seen my own mother die. So death does not scare me, and I don't find it cruel.

After a while, hope becomes far more abusive. I have always been pretty good at partitioning my life. By that I mean, compartmentalise things, categorise them accordingly. Maybe you are good at that too, but I found myself to be exceptionally good at it. I could separate universes in my own world. I could deal with one aspect of my life but not let it interfere with another aspect in any way. I think that spoke of focus, and allowed myself to devote to whatever I really put my mind to.

From an early age in my life, I had decided that the best form of defence was attack. I had resolved that taking on the world and living life to the fullest would be my approach in life. Come rain or sunshine, that would be my mindset, and I would keep this approach constant whether I would go through happy days or if I'd be met with setbacks and problems.

I hope I do not come across as being flawless and infallible, since I too, without a doubt had my moods, my memories and, of course, my mistakes. When I tell you about the shiny side, I am not going to gloss over the darker parts. I will lay it all bare; that's the reason I had decided to write this book in the first place.

So, as it turned out, I decided that I was not going to give a damn about what people thought or said about me. You know that Mark Twain quote: "Dance like nobody's watching; love like you've never been hurt. Sing like nobody's listening; live like it's heaven on earth." I lived to embody that. And even now as I write my book down piece by piece, I am not scared or anxious about your judgements or what you think about me. I am going to continue with this book, and I know you or will say and think what you want to, anyway. Hence, it feels stupid to me to censor myself here.

So anyways, we continue with my life. My early years were just awful. It was a lot for a child of that age to experience and process. Without a doubt. Even though I conquered in my own ways and made out strong, I think I wouldn't wish that torture upon anybody else.

In order to escape from the agony of my reality, I made use of my partitioning quality. I would split myself into different characters. It was the only way to evade the kind of pressure life was thrusting at me from all directions. I hide parts of myself that would later emerge as distant personalities, sometimes with different names.

Eventually, I realised something, and at this point it may seem like a simple enough solution, but back then it was a revelation. I realised that it wasn't me that was wrong, it was my evil foster father, Moore. He had always made me feel like I had deserved to get the punishment I'd receive. That was just how it worked with every kid, I thought. With the constant pattern of abuse, I was constantly encouraged to think what I face is a necessary part of life. I would think how my foster father wanted me to think, that yes, I needed discipline. That I must be worthless, otherwise why would this be happening to me?

All of this had been crippling for my self-esteem, but I hung on and carried as strongly as I could. I couldn't let myself be hardened, even though I was battered and bruised from all the beatings. I didn't want to think that I was weak. Some resistance was there within, and I latched on it. I would think to myself that I am a master, and made sure that I loved myself because no one else was loving me. In that capacity, I raised my own self. And I think I did a pretty good job.

Chapter 5: Remembering Friends

I remember going with my friend Joseph Chung and his parents to the Dakara Creek. The cool, clear water sparkling in the hot sun shone like a million pieces of amber transported from Aladdin's cave, falling against the glittering white sands. I was mesmerised. Smell the earthly smell of the steaming roads drying in the blazing heat filled me with relief after a short pounding burst of rain. Everything seemed paradisical that day.

I distinctly remember the sweet taste of a ripe mango picked from Mr Smith's tree. The feel of the sticky juice as it ran down my chin is still etched in my memory. I remember how it joined drop by drop by golden drop onto the patchwork of other stains on my shirt; I couldn't care less about it. We would spend our days eating Tambrine with salt, Bananas, Pineapple, Guavas, Ginnips, Star Apple, Monkey Apples, plus so many of the different fruits found in that part of the world. We could never get used to the immense sweetness and pleasure of those fruits.

As a small boy growing up in a tropical country, one of my favourite times of the year was Easter. That was not because of any religious significance, but because there would be so many different things to do.

The Shaved Ice Man on Sundays would arrive with so many different flavours and colours. We would battle summer with that cool dessert. We would also eat Brown

Betty's ice cream, a big, tasty, juicy burger from Demico House and have walks from Kingston Seawall all the way to Liliendaal, watching the big ships as they sailed out into the Atlantic Ocean. We would be left wondering just where they were going to and wished we were on it, going somewhere, anywhere.

Though I lived in the countryside, I was a city boy at heart. Urban lifestyle had made a home in me, given that I went to school in the city. Then after school and between breaks, my friends and I would travel all over the city, surveying, exploring; experiencing life.

One time me and my other friends Patrick Adams, Clifford Tudor, Orin Canterberry and Earl Brown went to the ocean. The tide was far out, but we decided that we wanted a swim, so we stripped down to our birthday suits, putting the clothes behind a rock and ran out into the sea.

We were having a whale of a time, when I just happened to look towards the shore and saw a Police Jeep pulling up towards our clothes. When someone is approaching your clothes when you're out for a swim, your heart just sinks automatically. You know that is never a good sign.

I shouted out to the others, "Look, look! The Police are taking our clothes."

We all then started running as fast as we could back to the shore with both hands covering our nether regions. As we reached the Police Jeep, we began pleading with the officer, "Please Sir, can we have our Boxers?" The driver drove around in the jeep and we chased him, continuously pleading. Another hundred metres he drove then stopped and gave us all our clothing back.

"What School are you boys from?" he barked. "St Barnabas, Sir," we all replied. The driver told them all to get into the Jeep and took them back to school. On our arrival, we were greeted by the headmaster, who had decided to make an example out of us right away.

As kids, while we were riddled with anxiety inside, we almost didn't move physically.

So the headmaster gathered the whole school to assemble, then proceeded to bench us (that meant a beating. Benching was our way of saying, make the boys bend over a desk, giving each one of them six lashings with a cane). That was a regular part of our school life. Someone or another would always be getting benched because of some misdemeanour.

So we were at the receiving end of it this time. While being beaten, the words added by our torturer, addressed to the whole school, were, "This is what you will get for skipping school if any of you wish to follow in their footsteps."

That was some unforgettable experience of humiliation. But of course, one that we can look back on today and laugh at.

Chapter 6: Market Days

Let me tell you an interesting thing about my early days and a peculiar part of my routine back then. This is of the time when I was under foster mother Clarice's care.

She would take me to the market before school. Now, for most children, or I guess it would be safe to say, for all children, school time is early in the morning, somewhere around 8. But early morning held a different definition for me. Early morning meant 4 am for me.

My foster mother would wake me up at four in the morning. See, it's still one thing to be woken up so early and another thing to do what she made me do. She would literally make me go outside and have an ice-cold shower from the forty-gallon oil drum that stood at the side of our house.

Now you're thinking, a forty-gallon oil drum? What was that doing outside your house, Michael? Well, we had it placed outside house because it could catch all the rainwater that ran down the guttering of the house.

I know that Guyana is warm and tropical throughout the year, but ice-cold water is... ice-cold. And 4 am anywhere in the world is a relatively frigid hour. I would be amazed when I'd watch my condensed breath from the cold water release. It was like I was smoking. It's a curious phenomenon for a child.

Regardless, that routine makes me feel like I was training to become a Navy SEAL or something. They undergo such rough training and drills.

I wasn't by myself in the shower. Clarice would be there and she would dry me before putting coconut oil into my hair. I remember the scent of that oil rising and whiffing into my nose as vividly as I remember the daily ritual. After that she would comb my black curly hair. No matter how old or young you are, dear readers, you know that there is no feeling in the world like getting your hair oiled and combed by your mother.

Can't say it for 4 am showers, but I sure did love the daily car rides to the market. They were accentuated due to the time of the day it was. I just loved the dawn chorus of the chirping, singing birds on the trees and in flight, that first light pouring in and nature blooming. Where I lived, geese were popular. They would fill the morning sky, going wherever they wished to migrate freely at that time of the day. Perhaps they were catching the early worms, just like me.

No matter how long I lived in the countryside I could never get tired of the horses. I also loved the sound clip-clop of their hooves as they made their way into the Capital, laden with fresh produce. One could just watch it all like a fly on the wall and never get bored.

Among the singing birds, quite distinct was the sounds of the house wren singing, and also the sound of the blue Saki or the Kissade bird. These are beautiful creatures, kinda like sparrows but more elegant, with their beautiful black, grey and blue feathers.

There's nothing like the hustle and bustle of the big city. The smell of fresh bread and cakes baking from Mr. Yip's baker shop added the olfactory pleasure to the sights… it all added to the scenery. If one could recreate that as a painting, what a rich painting it would be.

I would sometimes have the red cake and ice puma milkshake. Yum yum, the taste of these commodities was heaven.

Believe it or not, I also loved to listen to the grown men talking politics and putting the world right. Funny thing, to hear that a child used to like listening to political gossip, but it was really such an amusing thing for me. The way they sometimes went about eagerly and sometimes so aloof about the politicians and matters of national state urgency. It was a spectacle, indeed.

Then there was the beep beep noise from the traffic because everybody wanted to just get through the crowd. It was as if if they never horned, they would never be able to pass.

And finally, how can I forget the human bustle? The vendors and the punters would always be looking for a bargain, inviting clients over loudly and with their lavish offers. The sound of all the different vendors shouting, "Come buy," or "Lime! buy your lime fresh lime here!" or their would be screams of "Get your..." added by fresh banga, red snapper, fresh juice, catfish caught today, or Boneless sharksteak.

These were the market days and I loved experiencing it every morning before school.

Chapter 7: Finding New Places

Between the age of six and nine, I was allowed to go to the market with my foster mother, Clarice. After I had helped her set up her stall, she would give me a dollar. Back in those days, a single dollar could buy you a lot of sweets. It was a lot of money for someone as young as I was.

I would then go to the National Museum, where they used to show movies on History and Nature. This was something I really used to enjoy. As a child, it's amazing how much movies can teach you. After this, I would return to the market and watch all the ferries and boats crossing the Demerara River. This felt meditative. On my way back, I would sometimes go for walks along different Streets of Georgetown, trying to educate myself on the city. This exploration meant learning new streets names, checking out churches, cinemas, parks, playgrounds and swimming pools.

By the time I was ten years old, I knew the city like a vicar knew my bible; thoroughly.

Because I loved reading, I was encouraged by my teacher Mrs Beaton to join the school library. It seemed like a nice opportunity, so I seized it. I read everything and anything I could get my hands on. That didn't appease my appetite, which was hungry for knowledge, so I studied the atlas of the world and all the different countries; their Oceans, mountains, seas, etc.

I never kept a book on me for more than four days. I never had to since I read all of them pretty quick. I would read by candlelight into the early hours of the morning. Then once I was done, I would return them back to the library and exchange them for another.

My foster mother would often tell me off for staying up so late, so as soon as she would be off to sleep, I would relight my candle and carry on reading. This was a regular part of my life.

When I had to take the cattle out to graze, I would always carry a book with me. I would settle down under a lamp post in the shade and read.

One day, I was so engrossed in my book I didn't realize that the animals had left the pastures and had gone out onto the highway. Boy, was that a disaster. Thankfully, the local police had taken them back to the pound, but when I reached home, I realized that I was in a lot of trouble.

Sure enough, later that night, Moore went to his room and gave out the most vicious beating I had ever received. I was in a real bad way by the following day.

At the back of the house in Liliendaal was a deep canal that grew water calaloo and grass, which was something that the pigs loved. Moore made me go into the canal and collect the calaloo and grass.

He would stand on the banks and watch me, then I would shout out to him that there were crocodiles in the waters. It was a shout I'd give out of fear, and Moore used to make so much fun of me!

Poor me though, I was bullied at home as well as at school. At school, it was by a boy named Ian Edwards. Everyone in the school was afraid of him. He loved to slap and kick me, take my lunch money and my bus fare.

One day after school, Ian had taken the bus fare off me and also given me a really good kicking. This meant I had to walk back home injured, which took a long time. The animals were waiting for me to take them out, plus all my other jobs on the list had to be done.

When I tried to explain to Moore about the bullying, he served me another severe one. He followed off by saying, "Here are your choices, you get beat up at school or get beaten up at home."

I felt so angry and that came out in the form of tears. I cried all night and I decided that the next day at school, all of this would come to an end.

I reached the school early the next day and waited for Ian to come. Soon as Ian was in sight, I ran at him and threw a right punch that knocked him off his feet. As soon as Ian got up, I promised him that we would finish this at the end of the day.

I carried on with the rest of my school day in peace and felt very pleased with myself. After school, a group of students had gathered on the Merryman's Mall for the showdown. I was ready for this, but would you believe it? Ian had fear written all over his face as soon as he saw me. The fight was on, though.

I threw the first hit and carried on hitting and punching as hard as I could. I was taking it all out on him. It wasn't long before Ian started to cry, shouting out, "SORRY, MICHAEL. I'M SORRY!"

I stopped, emptied Ian's pockets, took all his money and went on my way. Ian never bothered me again.

Let me now tell you about Joseph Chung. He was a friend of mine who had made a song called I Row the Boat Ashore and Mash Up the Eddoe.

During break time at school, Joe and I would go to the market to look under the stalls for money that had been dropped. We would find ten cents, twenty cents or even a dollar sometimes. This would help us buy snacks from this particular vendor outside school, and boy, did she sell some tasty snacks. Things like egg balls, tamarind balls, chicken foot.

Sometimes we would go to the church yard and chat with Father Percy. He was a very nice man, a true man of the cloth. Every time we went to him, we returned with interesting stories.

In school, as a student, I was a smart, clever student. I would write down everything I was taught and absorbed knowledge quite efficiently. I was also a practical joker in the class, though. From time to time, this would get me into trouble. The teacher would make me stand in front of the class and take over the teaching, but because I did such a good job of teaching (since I was a clever student), the teacher would tell me to go back and stand on my desk. This would just bring the devil out of me, though. Fun times.

After school, I would go to a cafe on Regent Street. I would put a few dimes in the jukebox and just chill, listening to some tunes before making my way home to reality – home where Moore and a thousand duties awaited me.

I hated Sundays since if I wasn't taking care of the animals, Clarice would have me cooking, sewing, and washing. While I was doing all this, I would hear my friends outside the house, playing football or cricket. I was never allowed to go outside and join them, not even for half an hour. This also made me angry.

Sometimes the cricket ball or football would land over in my yard, so Moore would send me to get the ball and bring it to him. Then he would cut it into small pieces and return it to me to throw over the fence back to the lads. They would shout and swear at me, thinking I did it. I would also receive threats they were going to give me a beating if I crossed paths with them.

These same boys happened to knuckle me on my head. This turned into a fight, but I was no match for them. I did not back down without a fight, though. I hurt them, so in the end, they left me alone.

Another job I had at the farm was to get grass for the cows and the rabbits' feed. I would survey the houses nearby; when I was done collecting, I would go onto the next village, then further afield to Camberville, then onto Kitty, making friends along the way. For this reason, I really enjoyed grass-collecting.

I would cut the grass, fill up my sacks, play around with my friends before returning home. Then, when I was asked why it had taken me so long, I would simply say, "I had to go real far to get this kind of grass."

For this rebellion, I would receive one hell of a beating, the worse ever.

You see, at one of the houses where I got grass from, there was a beautiful girl named Abigail. I liked her a lot but didn't have the courage to tell her. But this particular day, as I arrived, she was outside, waiting. She asked if I would like a cold drink. I said, "Yes, please," but very sheepishly. When she returned, she gave me my drink along with a note. I drank my juice then read the note. It said that she really fancied me and asked if they could go steady. I was blown away.

By this time, she had gone back into the house and was watching from her window. I waved to her to come down. She must have taken four steps at a time, for she was there within seconds. I confessed my feelings to her that from the first time I saw her, I had liked her, but was always too shy to say it.

We then went and found some shade under a tree and sat chatting and laughing, even stealing a kiss here and there. Before I knew it, time flew by. It was now eight o'clock. What was more, I hadn't gotten any grass.

I got very scared, said goodbye and off I went. I was petrified to go home, so I went to my friend Grandolph's house and told him the situation. Grandolph instructed me to sit down, gave me a drink and something to eat, and told me to stay there for the night. Only, I had to sleep in the chicken pen.

At six o'clock the next morning, Grandolph's granny came in to feed the chickens and got a fright of her life to find me fast asleep there. I had to explain to her what had happened. She said, "Don't worry, child. I will take you home and speak to Moore. Everything will be alright."

I hoped to God everything would indeed be alright.

Chapter 8: One Hell Of A Beating

Later that morning, granny filled me with assurances and brought me back home. Moore was in the garden sowing seeds. I strolled past Moore with a shy hello, and went straight inside. Under normal circumstances, he may have probably followed me and given me a whooping, but Grandolph's granny's presence saved me. She was talking to Moore as I observed them surreptitiously. The moment I found them share a laugh, I felt safe enough and so decided to attend to the animals and returned later in the evening.

I washed, had supper, and took myself off to bed, but something told me this was not the end. That I was not going to be let off the hook so easily. Upon the suggestion of my intuition, I slipped under my bed and fell asleep there. It was just past midnight when I heard Moore enter my room, locking the door behind him. He went over to the bed, turning it upside down, grabbed and beat me with a garden hose. My skin was busted, broken, bruised. I was in so much pain that I couldn't even sit or lay down. I cried with the pain all night.

The next morning I had no choice but to carry on with my jobs. While I was out collecting eggs, I could hear Moore boasting to my Sue how he had given the 'little red skunk' a beating that I would never forget. Tears started rolling down my face, but I carried on with the chores. What could I have even done in response?

I could not for the life of me figure out why I was mistreated so badly. As much as I tried to think about it, I was never wise enough to understand. As a young boy, you start thinking it is somehow your own fault, which messes with you mentally. My self-esteem, in this case, was getting battered.

Moore then shouted at me to get the wheelbarrow and go to the seashore and barrow some sand to make a footpath in the front garden. Now, remember this was a very hot country, and I was being sent off midmorning, and I am still in excruciating pain from the beating. I set off still because I didn't want to be beaten any further. The pain mixed with the raging heat tormented me as I walked to the seashore. Another threat was that it is illegal to remove the sand from the shore, but I had to do it since these were orders from Moore.

So, I spent the next five hours going back and forth, wheelbarrowing the sand.

From time to time, some of my friends would see me and help with the load and give me moral support, all of which I was grateful for. So, although this was a punishment in a strange way, I enjoyed it for I got to have a laugh and a joke with my friends. Life has a strange way of compensating for your aches, I feel.

There were many more beatings to come because I just could not stay away from Abigail for long. I remember one day I had made plans for us to go to the cinema. After having such a lovely time, I had to return home, which I did but late, but for that, life compensated yet again with another round of vicious beating from Moore. I think I took it like a champ, yet again.

At this point, I was becoming tough to it all. That happens. Whatever you are overexposed to, you get used to it. This aspect of human nature works both in our favour and opposition. If you receive too much love, you will start taking it lightly too. This is because your emotions are getting accustomed to it. The same thing applies to beatings; your body starts getting accustomed to it.

I had also started to take self-defence and boxing classes at this point, though I remained too small and frail to take on Moore. To take it one step further then, I decided to join Charles Wong Karate School at the YMCA after school on a Monday and Wednesday.

I loved every minute of it. These classes were helping me boost my confidence. There's nothing too mysterious about it. When you are practising martial arts and fighting moves, it helps your body align with your mind. Synchronicity develops in your actions. You are in better command of your body, and that makes you feel good. As a result, your confidence grows.

I signed up for boxing lessons that an ex-Guyana boxing champion Cliff Anderson was providing. I learned about it when he came into our school to give a talk.

I was hooked on boxing, and this was to stay with me for the rest of my life. More on that later.

Back at home, farm errands and beatings weren't all that I experienced. I had two favourite dogs; a Labrador called Ginger and a mongrel named Cidimava. I had found them dumped at the side of the road when they were still pups. I brought them home and bottle-fed them until they were strong enough to feed themselves properly. They were lovely dogs. I adored them with all my heart, and we therefore formed a bond. They would follow me around where ever I went. I just hated it when I was made to lock them up.

But I would bring them out with me when I went to attend the cows in the fields. Their exuberance – the way they jumped and frolicked about – told me they loved it. And as a result, so did I. Ginger and Cidimava became a source of joy for me. Outdoors, we did everything together. Even when I went for a swim, so did the two dogs. After playing in the water, they would lie by my side, and together, we'd be drying off in the sun.

But of course, my happiness was not going to last, was it.

Back at the house, we had a room that was used to house the ducks. Several pods had been set up there for the ducks to brood on and hatch their eggs. One night, the dogs managed to sneak out and found their way to this duck house. They are all the eggs and killed some of the ducks and the ducklings. As soon as I found out, my heart fell already. When Moore discovered what my dogs did, he went mad. He called me and ordered me to go and shoot the dogs.

I pleaded with him, begged him, "Please, please don't kill them," I pled, but my pleas went unheard.

My lovely dogs were shot, and I was left to bury my two best friends, muttering to myself, "What a cruel fucking bastard." As I continued to bury the dogs, I felt more and more distraught. I was sobbing on and on and cursing in-between my cries, under my breath. I repeated over and over, "I hate him, I fucking hate him."

The next day, Moore went out and brought five new pups. You'd think he'd have been soft enough to get them for me, but no. He added another ten pups over the coming months, and would feed them all blood. His purpose was to make them vicious; they were not to be treated as pets. They were to be fed, watered, and locked away during the day.

It's a strange law of the world. Even though these were the same creatures as my two lovely dogs, they were feral. Why? Because they were missing the strongest ingredient that could make them softer and friendly: love. They were simply deprived of love and nurtured to be wild. And so, they grew to be just that.

I was given the job of feeding and unlocking the dogs and leave them out that just before going to bed. They were the protectors of the farm at night, the night watchmen. Hungry for intruders and savage against them.

All around the yard and the gate Moore had set up an alarm system of his own by running strings five-foot-high then connecting a large bell that ran into Moore's room. He had a cutlass wall sharpened, and his my gun at the ready for anyone who dared to enter his property to try to rob it. It was his life stock, and he was protecting it with all his life. No robbers would dare challenge Moore.

Or would they?

Chapter 9: The Robbery

One evening at around eight, I had just finished doing the last job of the day. I had my wash and got ready for bed, typically tired, as I was every day. I decided to have a little treat before letting the dogs loose, and asked Clarice for milk and biscuits for a nice little doze-off. My foster brother Lewis was also getting ready for bed.

When there was no response from Clarice, Lewis decided to check up on her. He was only gone for a second when he came running back into the bedroom, screaming, "There's a man in the living room with a big gun to mummy's head!" Hearing this, I told Lewis to climb out of the bedroom window and run, which is just what we both did.

But out of the frying pan and into the fire. Upon getting to the gate, we both saw another man with a gun. It was dark, and so we decided to take our chances. We both turned around, our hearts in our throats and ran to the front gate.

The man was shouting, "GET BACK HERE," but neither did he fire off his gun, nor did we stop running. We ran as fast as our legs allowed us. Off we went and came upon the local rum store that went by the name of Spot. We ran inside and started telling the elders what was happening.

Right then, all of us heard two successive gunshots and froze for a second.

Two of the elders, Fredrick and John, said they would go and see what was happening. They were gone but not for too long. Upon their safe return, they asked us to call for the police.

Lewis and I were too scared to return home that night, so we spent the night at the store and face whatever waited at the farm.

The following day we both were told that the men who had shown up at our house the night before had been bandits and had taken all the money and jewellery in store. Another thing was that Moore had been beaten to a pulp and was now in the hospital.

The most unfortunate of all, though, was that Clarice had gone missing.

Fortunately enough, she was found about two miles away from the house but in a state of shock. We arranged for him to be taken to the hospital. She didn't speak for two days.

Moore needed thirty-two stitches in his head and lost significant loads of blood.

The two gunshots that we heard were fired by the neighbour Jason three houses down after hearing a cry for help. While he came to the rescue with good intentions, the kind man was shot in the leg by one of the bandits. He also had to be taken to the hospital, the same one as Clarice and Moore.

Lewis and I went to see Clarice in the hospital and she finally started talking again. She informed us about what had happened. When the shots were fired, she ran through the back gates, jumped into the canal, and swam away to safety. Call me sick, but as bad as the incident was for all, I was quite glad that I no longer had to deal with Moore at home. In fact, I don't think you'll find me sick for feeling like that since Moore deserved the karma of what he made me go through. And to put it on record, I did not think Clarice,

Lewis and I deserved the trauma we faced. And really, I enjoyed Moore's presence for not just that I was no longer getting beaten, but because of the enjoyment I got to have. So, while Moore recovered at the hospital, I got to play with my friends day and night. The best part about this was, my friends were allowed to stay over to keep me company.

It indeed was as that idiom goes, when the cat is away, the mice will play.

To tell you the truth, I wasn't all innocent about it. My mischief snuck in here and there; for instance, when it was time for them to return home, I would use my "But I'm scared" card. It worked every time and so that Clarice would let them stay.

Chapter 10: Changes Were To Come

After the robbery, Moore spent a short time in the hospital, and he then returned home soon.

Upon his return, he was on a mission and decided to make a lot of changes around the house. Metal bars were fitted at the windows and doors, making the house look more like a prison. No one was allowed to visit indoors. He treated everyone like a suspect, eyeing them suspiciously and never talking straight. In his head, he always believed he knew the bandits included at least one of them.

If ever that person walked past Moore, he would spit and devour him. He hated everyone, and in return, everyone started hating him with a passion, especially my neighbours. This hatred was going to cause a lot of trouble for Moore... and of course, in turn, for me too.

And so it happened one day. The lads were playing a game of cricket outside our house when the ball went into Moore's yard. The chid next door, their youngest son Barnard shouted out to me, "Can we please have our ball back?"

If it were up to me, I'd have given it and joined them even. But Moore had heard the boy and told me not to move, so I had to stay put.

But Bernard was having none of it. He climbed over the gate and got back his ball. When Moore saw him, he chased Barnard, who stopped and threw a bicycle sprocket at

Moore. It caught Moore on the head, splitting it open. There was blood everywhere.

This was in the days before anyone had telephones, so they couldn't call for an ambulance. Moore tore off his shirt, used it as a bandage, and then made his way to Rupert Craich Highway. He managed to flag down a car that gave him a lift to Pleasance Police Station, which was about five miles away.

Later that evening, Moore returned in a police car, and they went round to next door where after a short time, Barnard was arrested. They took him to a Juvenile Centre, where he stayed for a few days then was released on bail. Everyone else at home was watching this play out curiously.

Because Moore's house faced where Barnard lived, a lot of name-calling started exchanging. A few weeks later, the case went to court in Sparadamm District of Pleasance.

I was called as a witness and had to tell my side of the story. I was so terrified, and the fright made me shake like a leaf.

I made my way to the stand. The Judge a very hard-looking woman. She asked me to tell the court my name. I tried to speak, but nothing came out of my mouth. When words did manage to come out, I sounded more like a squeaky mouse than a human. I mean, I couldn't even say, "Michael," out loud. That's how my state was

The Judge shouted at me, asking me to use my male voice. I somehow managed to speak, but it was not a nice experience for me in the end.

I don't know how but Bernard's family got the money for the best lawyers. They ripped into Moore and tore him to bits and won the case hands down.

Bernard walked up to Moore and me and laughed in our faces before leaving the court.

As you can imagine, Moore was not happy, and he sure let me know just how unhappy he was when we got home. Just as Moore was getting a length of garden hose, our next-door neighbours were just arriving home. Moore didn't care for anyone who watched; he was putting on a display. Possessed by rage, he continued with the most horrendous public beating. He beat me so severely and kept screaming, "THIS IS WHAT YOU GET WHEN YOU SIDE WITH THE ENEMY," and called me a little skunk.

Crowds began to form, watching me take the beating of my life. I was crucified in front of everyone, yet not one person tried to stop it or help me.

After the beating finally stopped, I got myself up, feeble and aching all over, onto an old tyre and sobbed my heart out, asking myself, 'Why? Why me?'

My body was all black and blue and swollen everywhere. I was in pain if I stood up, if I sat down, if I lay down. I know I keep saying every time about the worst beating of my life, but this one really was. It had successively been getting worse for me, in fact.

But I still had to do my jobs, there was no excuse. I had to do them despite being all black and blue. My swollen body hurt with every step I took. The pain was unbearable, especially when I tried to bend and milk the cows or collect my eggs. It seemed like my bones were being crushed. Yet, I just had to grin and bear it. There was no one I could ask for help, and nowhere I could go.

I can recall that my teacher once asked me what I would like to be when I grew up. I answered with confidence I would like to be in the army, Police Force, The Prison Service, and the fire brigade. The teacher told me that I couldn't be all of those things. "You can only do one," Miss said to me.

I replied, "I can do them all, and I can assure you that I will." At that time, it was only talk. By the time I was sixteen, I was taking part in Karate and boxing matches and training hard every day.

In the mornings, I would do road work with my now new coach and an Olympic Champion, Judge Sealy.

Chapter 11: No Regrets

Despite all the ill treatments, beatings and name-calling, I still learned how to smile and be polite to everyone. People thought that this came easy to me, but you can bet it didn't. It took a lot of work. Not the kind of work that I did at the farm. This type of work was purely mental; I had to be in control of my mind.

I had learned that I must find a positive outlet for all this pent-up anger or it would destroy me given all the shit I had to put up with. I couldn't continue the cycle of abuse. I pledged this much with myself. Whatever Moore did, it was probably because he was abused as a child too, so that was the only way he knew how to communicate. He had to find his catharsis through physically torturing me, but I knew I wouldn't do anything like that. Often this happens that you end up becoming who you hate. But I knew I wouldn't become another Moore.

These resolutions meant that I had to find another way to channel all that anger. I had to grow up fast or die young.

The life I knew and was living was not the life for me; I knew that much too. I knew faith had something else, something bigger in store for me, because I was a good man. I knew I didn't belong and knew I had potential. I felt trapped, but also felt very fortunate for the obstacles that I had to deal with. They taught me things much quicker and more ardently than a normal child. My harsh upbringing prepared me for life. I felt myself grow older for my age and more mature compared to others.

I still didn't hold any ill feelings towards anyone. It was like I could see clearly that there should be no room in my heart for regrets. I was grateful for the harsh lessons that I had learnt, because gratitude goes a long way. Regret, rage or disappointments, anguish, hate, all these things carry a negative strand about them. They rot you from the inside, given the energy these emotions contain. This is why I constantly struggled to be better than such negativities.

I remember how one night, after yet another hard beating, I had gone under the stairs where it was quiet and dark. I needed that dark solitude, needed to sit there crying and shaking. There may have been anger in me at first, but like every time, it dissolved. Soon, a sense of calmness would descend upon me, just as it did every single time.

Chapter 12: The Mystery Woman

At this stage, I must have been around the age of nine when I came across a woman whose name was Genevieve for the first time ever. I became intrigued by the enigma and mystique around her.

She would come to see Clarice at the stall. Clarice in return would give her money for food and her cigarettes. This was the extent of her interaction with Clarice.

I don't know who she was, but I would get a weird feeling because she would just stare at me. When she would speak to me, she would call me by my middle name, David. No one called me David, I was Michael for all those who knew me.

Genevieve had another bizarre habit. She would always tell me that she loved me, and then would go on to light up a cigarette. She always did this, after which she would turn and walk away from me.

I still had no idea who the hell she was, but my curiosity would spike every time. I eventually gave in and went ahead to ask Clarice about her. She told me that she was just her friend, but that was not a satisfactory answer. There was never any reason why I shouldn't believe that, though while I wouldn't be entirely convinced, I wouldn't push it either.

As if it couldn't get more mysterious, this woman used to turn up at my school, too. She was known as the 'crazy woman'. As is the stigma with people labelled crazy, she would be a target of bullying. My friends and I would throw old fruits at her and shout all kinds of curses. We would laugh at her as she wiped her face.

Looking back at it now, this is not something I am proud of. But then again, we all have our hooliganism when we're young.

Another crazy thing was, before Genevieve turned away, she always mouthed the words, "I love you, son." I never took that seriously, and thought of it as some kind of twisted behaviour. Older women went around calling little kids 'son', so there didn't seem too much to dig. Sometimes she would say, "David, I love you," but would just always turn away after saying that. This would leave me wondering how did she know my name?

Sadly, one of these fruit-throwing days turned out to be the last time I was to see Genevieve alive. The mystery woman died a mystery.

Chapter 13: The Penny Finally Dropped

One morning while I was helping Clarice, she told me that she needed to speak to me. She apparently had something important to tell.

It really felt important when she took me to a nearby café, ordered my favourite snack which was cream and jello. This was all in preparation for what she was about to tell me. I was starting to get nervous too because she never did things like that. I mean, she treated me sweetly, but I had a feeling this was something huge.

Clarice began to tell me that she and Moore were not my birth parents and went on to explain how she had come about being my Foster mother. Keep in mind that up until this point, I had not known that I was adopted. I always thought these two were my birth parents. She was sobbing as she narrated it all to me, clearly realising the intensity of the confessions.

The cream and jello suddenly turned sour for me. The news came as a terrible shock to me. I couldn't compute it all immediately, but everything started to make sense to me as I listened to her. The different surname, the different skin colour, the way I didn't fit into the Moore family. I could now understand it all, the reason for why Moore treated me the way he did while Lewis was not subjected to such horrors.

With the truth still sinking in, Clarice then informed me that the woman who came to see me at her stall was, in fact, my real mother. This made my chest ache and sent tremors through my body.

The anger that had built up until that point came gushing out. I was livid, and in that state, I shouted at Clarice, "WHY HAVEN'T YOU TOLD ME THIS BEFORE? I HAVE

TREATED HER SO BADLY!" I was sobbing at this stage, and in-between the sobs, I just kept asking why, why, why? That was not the end to her confessions. There was more Clarice had to tell me. With tears running down her face, she continued divulging that that there had been an accident involving Genevieve. She couldn't meet my eyes when she told me that my biological mother died in that accident. "WHERE? WHERE?" came my immediate response, shouting. It happened at the junction of Camp Street and Regent Street, Clarice told me.

Without another word, I jumped up and ran hell for leather to Camp Street. To my horror, right there on the ground, I saw his mother lying dead on the road. They were just about to cover her up with a white sheet. Blood pooled all around her. I felt hysterical.

I just couldn't control my tears, as well as the anger that had welled up inside him. I cried and cried in the deepest anguish I had ever experienced. The worst of Moore's beatings did not hurt me this much.

When I eventually calmed down, everything seemed to fall into place. That night, back at home, I fired questions at Clarice. Why this? Why that? How come this? Why not this? Who, when, how, why? On and on I went asking.

Clarice had to tell me that my mother had suffered from mental illness and refused help from anyone. She went on to tell me that he wasn't alone, that he had four big sisters and a big brother who still lived in Guyana. The mother in law of my elder sister Irene was being paid to look after my mother.

I was then handed the address of a woman called Elsa, who lived in the rich part of Georgetown in a village called Brickdam in a large white detached house.

So later that day, I took it upon myself to find the location. I got there, went up to the door and rang the bell. The door was opened by a very smartly dressed European woman with silver hair. I told her all about who I was, and straight away, she asked me to come in.

We sat in a posh parlour, drinking tea and talking about everything that I had learned recently.

The woman told me how very sorry she was for my loss, but assured me not to worry as everything was taken care of. Elsa gave me a phone number that belonged to my real grandma in Montreal, Canada. So off I went to the telephone exchange on Waters Street and placed a collect call to my grandmother. I spoke to her and explained about my mother and how she had met her death.

My grandmother was saddened. She told me that she was going to make plans to come to Guyana to attend the funeral. "But there isn't time for that. You see, in Guyana, it is so hot they have to bury the bodies as soon as possible," I told her. Therefore, grandma thought it wise to not return to Guyana. As for Elsa, she wouldn't want to see me ever again. She never answered the door every time I sent her letters or telegrams. My biological grandma so apart from me that there wasn't really anything else I could do.

My head was full of different things; feelings, thoughts, etc. The hurt he felt due to being betrayed, cheated by all the lies I had been told. I had been cheated from knowing the fact that I actually had a family, real flesh and blood. I was grieving the loss of my mother, of mistreating her too.

Every time I stopped still and thought of my mother, I could see her face, her caring eyes, her soft pink lips as they mouthed, I LOVE YOU. Even though they all called her crazy, despite her madness, she did not forget me. Despite the distance, she did not stop loving me.

No one had ever said I love you to me before, and now it was too late to appreciate the only one who did. She was gone, was all alone in that cold horrible morgue with no one willing to claim her.

She had six children, yet she meets her Maker all alone. She was left in the morgue for months as they waited for someone to claim her body but no one did. I went there every day to see her, asking if anyone had claimed her, but was told, no not yet. Every single time.

On one of these days as I went to see her, one of the workers grabbed me and asked if I was family and why no one had claimed her.

This was to be my last visit because the government had to take action. They sent her on her final journey all alone with no dress, no shoes, no flowers. Not one single flower was spread on her as she laid down to rest, and that too, in an unmarked grave paid for by the government.

I cried for Genevieve, I cried a lot. When she needed me the most, I denied her! I am not only talking about her visits to the stall or school. I am talking about when I was asked by the worker, "Do you know her? Are you related? Are you family" My reply was, "No, I don't know her."

This is something I will have to live with for the rest of my life.

In the weeks that followed, Clarice had the chance to tell me everything she knew about my mother and my family. How she came to be in Guyana, what happened to my big brother Anthony. Everything came together like a jigsaw puzzle. The pieces fit in perfectly. Finally, I came to see things through Clarice's eyes and realised all the sacrifices that she had made to foster me. It couldn't have been easy for her, and I wish I could say knowing all of this made reconciliation better, but it didn't.

As for that selfish, cruel, mean bastard of a husband of hers, that man Moore, he had not one drop of respect for my mother, me, his wife, or anyone. Moore had children everywhere with different woman, but all Clarice had really wanted was a child of her own. Although I wasn't her actual child by birth, I was a child she could call her own. She heard me call her mummy for many years, and that was all she really wanted.

It was to her that I wrote the Mother's Day cards to. It was to her that I showed love to. All the respect I gave her made her just so happy. So this was a time that I learned to be grateful for the mother I still had, though she was a foster one.

Clarice wouldn't let that bastard of a husband spoil it for her. After all, she was his wife but in name only. It was unfortunate really that she was the laughing stock of the village, but Clarice didn't care. She had little me, and she brought me up all on her own without any help.

I could and still have nothing but admiration for her for all that she had done for me.

Chapter 14: A Letter To My Mum

Dear Mum,

I've been thinking about you and about what your life must have been like around the time I was born.

You had no family or friends supporting you just because you chose to live your life differently. You must have had faced such a hard time trying your best to bring up two young boys in a foreign country. You must have been exhausted in such heat. Making ends meet every single day must have been such a toil.

As a white woman in Georgetown, you must have had experienced some terrifying times. You must have stuck out like a sore thumb. They might not have let you go off easy for that. From buying groceries to walking on the streets back home, peoples' stares alone might have discomforted you. Since I have also experienced how the people in Georgetown operate, having received the worst of it in some ways, I can relate with you on some level. But we don't compare really, since I have been on the other side of the fence.

I know what they say, that when you face challenging times on the regular, you get conditioned to it. But there's no way of knowing how much that hollows you on the inside.

There's no way of knowing how your hardships may have accelerated each day.

Conceiving two mixed-race children with no sign of a father must have been very lonely and scary. You must have felt so rejected. I try to, but I cannot really imagine the burden on your shoulders, dear mother. You are so brave for standing up to the times and hustling regardless.

For years I saw you on the streets and knew of your existence, but never knew who you really were. I was unaware of your true relation to me, but let me please say that I had my curiosity. I wondered why you looked at me the way you did, about how you called me David.

I remember when I was with friends out playing. You came along, but we always shouted and threw rotten fruit at you. We laughed at you as you wiped your face while you just stood there and took all the abuse. It breaks my heart now to think about it. It wrenches me just to think of how before turning away, you always mouthed the words, 'I love you, son.'

I never knew you were my mother until much later on in my life. How unfortunate that the truth came to me with your death. To this day, the way I treated you back then haunts me. I believe it will continue until the day I die.

But while I am here, I want you to know just how very, very sorry I am for how I treated you. To be a lone, struggling mother away from your own child for years and then getting mistreated on top of that when you visit your son. It must have hurt you so incredibly much in so many different ways.

No matter what happens now, I will always keep you in my heart. I will love you until I love and pray that you can now rest in peace in death. I wish that death compensates for all that you suffered in this life.

From your ever-loving son David Decosta

Chapter 15: Big Brother Anthony S Decosta

My elder brother Anthony was sent to the St Johns' Basco Orphanage for boys in Plisance on the East Coast of Demerara.

At first, he was distraught and broken-hearted. He found it challenging to settle in and adjust to his new surroundings with complete strangers. He was not used to it all, and of course, his mother and his brother weren't there. He was all alone. He had gotten used to having both of us there. Unlike me, he remembered our family, however small it was.

But now, he was surrounded by a horde of little boys of all colours, races and creeds. There were also Vicars and Nuns who set out the rules and set up your schedule. There were timings for everything, like when to eat, when to sleep, when to wake up, when to go to church. Everything was planned and over-organised. He was told when to do his chores and when he was allowed to play. All of this took time for him to get used to. He had not been used to such restrictions, after all.

Sunday was a day of worship but also a day for family visits. They also took the children out for the day. Treated them to a ride into the city, for ice cream, sweets, even the snow cone.

You'd think that Sundays were something that Anthony enjoyed, but no. Sunday fleeted away for poor Anthony without any real joy. Week after week, month after month, year after year, because no one ever came to see poor little Anthony. In that regard, he was like me, since nobody came to meet me either at Clarice's place. But you can at least say that Anthony didn't get beaten. To say it was all bad would be a lie, but to say it was all good would also be a lie.

Regardless, all this loneliness made him feel furious towards our mother. She had given up on him, he thought. He was angry at being dealt such a shitty life. Not only was he mad with our mother, but he was also angry at the world, at God, at his life.

Then one day, out of the blue, Anthony discovered something strange. He was playing with a little Indian boy, and they got chatting. The boy told Anthony about another little boy who lived in Georgetown near his family with the same surname Anthony's – meaning DeCosta. Now, Anthony was fully aware that he had a little brother that lived around there, so he asked the little Indian boy to ask his grandmother if he could go and see the lady who lived at this place. This lady was Clarice. Anthony wanted to pay a visit and to find out whether this boy was indeed his younger brother, Michael.

And so it went, it turned out that yes, it sure was his brother; me. Anthony was thrilled and happy about this news. So a meeting date was set. You can pretty much guess which day Anthony wanted to select.

Sunday. We were decided to meet on a Sunday. Anthony first had to attend service, so he sat near the front, but he was aware that I had already arrived and was sitting near the back. Anthony was just too excited. He kept looking behind him and waving at me all throughout the service.

As soon as the service was over, he ran towards me, and I ran towards Anthony. We met each other for the first time in what felt like forever and threw our arms around each other. Neither of us wanted to let go. We hugged so tight and for so long, it seemed like an eternity passed at that moment. And that was the beginning of us getting to know each other. It was almost from scratch, since we were both not what Anthony remembered us together as.

Finally, Anthony had his brother back, and so did I. For me, it was like I finally had a protective figure. We would now meet on Sundays. Every Sunday, we would meet and fly a kite, go to the beach, eat ice cream and would sit and chat and laugh.

Oh my God. This felt so good for both of us. It was as if it was at this point that life had actually begun. Both of us were experiencing real family properly for the first time.

If I think about it, it won't be wrong to say that the orphanage has a lot to do with the way Anthony is today. Fifty-seven years have elapsed, and he still finds it so very hard to trust and love people. When I say love, I mean real, deep love – that passionate, head over heels kind of love where you give your heart fully to another person. He still finds it hard to care genuinely. He finds it hard to let go and have a good scream and shout and tell someone – anyone – how he truly feels.

There are a million and one questions that Anthony wants to ask. I can see it in his eyes. When young children are put into care, they are supposed to be cared for, looked after. It was supposed to be like a family, if not better, but it was far from that. The feeling of family should not have been craved in that place by him. In place of God, where your teachers were nuns, a part of God, and the priest were men of God, Anthony especially should have felt safe. It should not have been yearned by me after being adopted.

Such things made us believe that only blood relations can really give that family feeling.

Anthony came to find out on a daily basis that the life at orphanage was mechanical and hollow. So far from the truth of all that he thought. The priests would be buggering the little boys, the nuns were raping boys. On top of that, they would make the boys believe that this is what God wants us to do!

I am talking about vulnerable children here who didn't know any better. They had no one to turn to, no one to tell, no one to complain to. At the same time, they also knew tha if they did manage to tell someone, they would not be believed. Such is the trend at many places still, you get victim-blamed and tagged as trouble makers. The trouble you are trying to escape, thus worsens. You end up in even more trouble then.

Lucky for Anthony, he was one of the few who got away with this most awful experience. I think he could have quite easily been anyway. He used to sleep with a knife under his pillow out of fear that he would be assaulted during the night. If anyone threatened him, his instincts would have taken care of it.

That being said, I truly believe no one should have to live their life in such fear and terror, never mind a child.

Unlike his little brother, me that is, Anthony could remember everything, the smell, the touch, the feel of his mother, all. He remembered the way she looked, the songs she loved, even the way she used to hold her cigarette as she sat looking out of the window. I think that is a treasure, to have these memories. For me all this was now just a distant memory, but oh, what I would give to have these images in my head.

Anthony would sometimes go and sit in the churchyard, looking up to the sky and recall the sermon he had once heard about God's love. He would think that if that was true, why was he here? If God loved him, why was He keeping Anthony deprived? It was days like these he would give his right arm to see his mother and little brother, if only for a short time. This is what loneliness can do to you.

Children of the orphanage were only allowed to stay there up to the age of sixteen. After that, they had to leave. So when Anthony reached the age of sixteen, one of the nuns, Claudette, got in touch with his family that lived in Canada.

One day, just like that, his grandmother appeared all the way from Canada, gracing Anthony's life, which was soon about to change.

Anthony loved how his grandmother looked like a little Angel with white hair. She had such a kind, caring face. To his utter surprise, she had come to take him to Canada.

75

The day he left Guyana, he was a mixed bag of feelings, really. Anthony was going to a place he knew nothing about, going to live among people he also knew nothing about.

Then there were all the goodbyes exchanged again. Anthony thought about me, his little brother who he was just getting to know. Knowing me, reuniting with me had made Anthony feel like he had a family again. But now, it was all being taken away. How could he say goodbye to the brother he had only just found out about and loved so much?

At the same time, somewhere deep inside him, there was joy too. It was the joy of starting anew and fresh. A clean slate.

The day finally came for Anthony to leave, and I was taken to see him and say his goodbyes. I believe this still remains as one of the hardest things either of us has had to do in this life. We hugged each other again, tighter than the very first hug after we had reunited.

Anthony was led away, put into the back of a car. He was crying like I had seen no man cry. With tears running down his face, soaking wet. As he watched from the back of the car window, I gave a run after the car, crying and shouting myself for him to come back. One of the screams I let out was, "Please don't leave me." It is cruel how words are being made to convey what is only meant to be felt. That experience was something else.

Anthony watched from the back of the car until I had disappeared from the view. I continued standing in the middle of the road until the car was just a tiny dot.

A few weeks later, I received my first letter from Anthony, one of many to come. This was the foundation of which our relationship grew to reach new brotherly heights. By that, I mean right up to this day. Even now, we keep in touch via phone, text and video calling.

Many years of being apart with miles of ocean between were about to change, though.

Anthony's grandmother, or our grandmother as I should say had gotten sick, and one of her final wishes was to see all her family together again.

Anthony had an Uncle Stanley whose wife's name was Mary. It was Mary who got in touch with me and explained and asked if it was possible for me to come. I could stay with them in their family home in Montreal, they told me. Anthony was living in Toronto.

I decided that I would go, and so I set about making plans, having made up my mind firmly.

When I arrived, I spent time with our grandmother. She was doing very poorly, but she insisted that I must go and find my brother, spend time with him. I made the call to Anthony, and so we decided that I would go and stay with him in Toronto for a few days. That is exactly what I did.

When I arrived in the early hours of the morning, my brother was there, waiting for me. We both hugged each other again, tightly, as the ritual went. We remembered each other from the past, but now we were grown men. The distance had done nothing to break our deep love apart.

After spending four days with my brother, I returned to see our grandmother, who was still very poor. This time she encouraged me to meet my cousin Mark and see the nightlife of Montreal and enjoy myself. I had a great time while I experienced these things. But as it always goes, the time came when I had to return back home. So I once again said goodbye to everyone and returned home.

It was a short time after I returned home that I got the news that our grandmother had passed away. God bless her soul. Amen.

Chapter 16: When I Turned 18

When I reached my eighteenth birthday I decided to join the Guyana Defense Force. No sooner had I made the decision, I was sent out for training into the jungle.

I left Georgetown for my six month Military training which was to be deep in the Amazon Jungle. We were about two hundred recruits all in all.

We boarded an ex-warship named JIMITO.

The excitement was extraordinary for all of us onboard as this was the first time any of us had been on a ship and the first time we had been out of Georgetown.

The first few hours on board were spent looking around the ship. It was like exploring, we were making friends and the food was plentiful. It felt like we were on some kind of holiday rather than going into the jungle to do the training.

Later that night, we were in the middle of the deep blue ocean when our ship developed some kind of electrical problem resulting in the loss of communication with the outside world, they announced that the engine was now failing. The Captain ordered for the anchors to be dropped, they were now stuck and at the mercy of the Atlantic Ocean. The Officers tried to make light of the situation to keep us all calm, assuring that we don't panic. Which, trust me, was difficult. Imagining getting stuck in the middle of a dark blue abyss that could engulf us at any moment, was a terrifying thought indeed.

There was a storm brewing now and the ocean was violent. Waves lifted and washed over the ship. We were being thrown around like rag dolls. The aggression of the ocean brought fear creeping into our veins as we saw what looked like impending watery grave for all two hundred of the recruits and staff.

This anxiety brought men down on their knees as they started getting sick everywhere. During the night no one went to sleep for they feared if they closed their eyes, it would be the very last sleep they get before they eternally close their eyes.

But the next morning things seemed to have calmed down. The ocean was like a giant gentle pond and the sun was out. All the recruits were now on deck feeling relatively better than last night when doom shone in their eyes.

It was later in the morning when someone shouted out that there was a boat in the distance, and our Captain let off the distress flare to let the boat know that we needed assistance.

After waiting for a while a trawler pulled up alongside the ship. The Captain of the trawler climbed aboard and chatted to the Captain of the JIMITO for a while then left.

It was to be another twenty four hours that they were stranded on the ship out in the big open Atlantic Ocean with men feeling sick, not only due to seasickness but also out of worry and anxiety. Time slows down when you are in dire need of it to hurry. I still remember feeling like I was stuck on the ocean for eternity before we were rescued.

I was laying on the top deck looking at the heavens above and was just so stunned at how many stars filled the sky. It looked like the sky was laden with pearls. I thought it was magical, perfect witchcraft.

Finally the next day a tugboat arrived to tow the JIMITO to its destination. There was a roar of excitement as everyone cheered and clapped at the sight of a tugboat that proved to be our savior. We were all thrilled to finally be moving and on our way again.

After its challenging and exhausting voyage on the ocean was over, it was now time for the ship to take on the stretched out windy rivers that would test its longevity and strength.

Everyone including me was very surprised to see actual native Indians on the riverbanks going about their daily lives, unaware of a vessel gaping at them. My imagination had only taken me so far when I had read about them in books so it was mind-blowing to watch them swimming in the river; the women with babies attached to their backs, cutting back bushes, smoke coming from small fires as they lit them up to put them to use.

This was the first sight and the first sounds of the jungle and I loved it. There were monkeys chattering and screeching in the trees, their sounds exhilarating the curious human inside me, and crocodiles napping lazily on the river banks. Not to mention the hundreds of species of birds, singing their individual songs in perfect harmony. You could see the otters bobbing about in the water and the speedboats that were zipping up and down the length of the rivers. I was beyond excited to see nature roaming around so freely there but the sight of the port filled me with a warm giddy feeling. I spotted some enormous ships and tankers there along with an old rusted sign which read WELCOME TO PORT KAITUMA. When the ship finally docked we were all allowed to get off the ship and by God, it was good to have our feet back on firm dry land after fighting the oceanic monsters for so long.

After a short time in the Force, I took up boxing again and quit the army. Clarice was not at all happy about this decision. She took it upon herself to speak to her niece named Nella who was a high ranking officer in the Police Force. She asked her to speak to Michael.

Nella agreed and met up with I soon after. She encouraged me to join the Police Force. I found her arguments strong, and her persuasion skills immaculate. And so, in the end, there I was, working to join the Police Force. Say what you may about me and my niceties, but one thing that's sure to perturb people is that I am a restless soul. And being a restless soul, I decided to leave the Force after serving just one year. There was no serious backlash this time.

I thought about what I wanted to do now, and finally resolved to join the Prison Service. It was going well, but yet again I became restless. After only a short stay there, I left that position too and went into the Fire Service.

While I was out and about, I bumped into an old friend. Remember Grandolph? His grandmother helped me by talking to Moore. He was now working as a gold miner and had just returned back to Georgetown from the jungle.

Grandolph said he could get me a job with him that could earn me one hundred US dollars a day. This is the kind of news back at home that makes your jaw drop. To give you an estimate, the Fire Service where I worked hard at only paid six hundred dollars a month. It would have thus made all the sense in the world for me to join my old friend at the mines.

The money sure was promised to pour in daily. I was more convinced when I saw just how much money Grandolph was making. He went on full throttle and spent that money like there was no tomorrow. I was eager for a lavish lifestyle too.

So, a meeting was set up for me to meet Grandolph's boss, and I was offered a job, confirming the one hundred dollars a day.

Yet again, I had to go and tell this to my foster mother, Clarice. I laid the entire plan before her, and yet again, she blew her top! Can I really blame her, though? She just wanted to see me make good of my life and rise up the ranks, to be a somebody. That meant settling somewhere, and as you can see, I'd been bouncing like a pinball here and there. As far as she was concerned, I had thrown away a very good job with prospects and was worried that I would end up like all the other lazy, good-for-nothing boys in the village.

This is where I realised I had to do my part. So I sat her down and assured her that I was not going to end up like them, and then I left.

The next day Grandolph and I caught a minibus to Sheriff Street. There we boarded an ex-British Army lorry, which was overloaded with food supplies for Derrick Leyoung miners company.

We left Georgetown later that night, making our first stop at Linden. Then we continued overnight on the road to Brazil. I wish I could say it was an easy trip, but it was the exact opposite; a hell.

The roads were in a terrible state, and with the recent heavy rainfalls, everything was flooded deep. There bizarre combination of mud and thick clay in the tracks caused the lorry to get stuck. More than once, we had to climb out and help push the lorry to get it back onto the road. It was as exhausting as it was unsettling.

We were up to our waist in mud, which soon dried on us luckily. But now, we were left looking like cardboard. There was nowhere for us to wash up or go to the toilet, so if we needed to go to the loo, we had to dig a hole and use that.

When we came to a river, we jumped into it as if our life depended on it. We would wash ourselves good, also fill up on our water supply. All this was a new experience for me, and I soon got the hang of it enough to enjoy it. I thought about all the money I would make, and that was enough to keep him going.

Chapter 17: Leaving Guyana

I returned to Georgetown after working in the mine for a year. By the time I had returned, the Christmas season had begun. The air was chilly, and my surroundings had a cheerful holiday glow to them. I made my way to the German Restaurant where I had ordered my food, and while waiting, I picked up the Guyana Chronicle newspaper. It was then that I came across an advert for Police Officers in Antigua. I hadn't got a clue where that was, but it caught my attention.

I sat down and thought about it and told myself that this was it, this was the way out of Guyana. I could be free and live my life the way I intend it to be. I made up my mind to see this opportunity through. As soon as I had eaten, I made my way to the Police headquarters. I stood astounded, eyeing the building with familiarity. I knew this place well, for this was where I had resigned from just the year before.

I was invited to do a written exam but was very nervous as the senior officers in charge were the same ones that had trained me. I was worried my past encounter with them might play against me.

Nevertheless, I passed the exams and was told to go to the local hospital for my medical, which I also passed. Soon after this, I was given a date to catch a flight to Antigua. All

I had to do was pack my bag and turn up at the airport. I could hardly believe my instant turn of good luck. This was it. I was finally leaving Guyana. It seemed everything was happening at the speed of light for me. It was an overwhelming feeling.

For the next few days, I took one final look around Georgetown. The day before my flight, I treated myself to a meal at my favourite restaurant. After that, I called the Botanical Garden Centre to buy Clarice a wonderful flower bouquet.

As I walked through the door, I saw her sitting in her rocking chair and went over to her. I handed her the flowers and kissed her on her head.

She told me that she did not want the flowers and that the only thing she wanted for me was to make something of myself. I was overcome with emotion. I knew this was the perfect moment to finally reveal the news to her. "Can we please just talk?" I asked her. "What about?" she shouted. "I have some really good news for you, and trust me, you are going to like it, and I think you're going to be proud of me." I told her that I am a Policeman again but just not in Guyana and that I have been offered a position in Antigua. "I leave tomorrow," I added. "You're lying!" she exclaimed, finding it hard to believe. I assured her that it was the truth. "No, I promise you, Mum, I'm not. It's the truth. I'm leaving tomorrow on the 747 to Trinidad, and then I catch a flight to

Antigua."

I was not prepared for what came next. Clarice began to cry as if someone had just given her a beating. In between all the sobs, she managed to say that she was indeed very proud of me. Clarice told me that she was also very pleased with me, for she knew that this was what I had always wanted since I was a small child. She said that she knew I wanted to leave this place because I had never fit in and was not happy here and never had been.

I hugged her passionately and promised that I would write to her as often as I could and assured her that I would also send her money every month.

After making sure that Clarice was feeling better, I went and got a shower. Put on my best clothes, went down to my favourite bar, SPOT 7, with some of my buddies for a farewell drink.

Sleep didn't come to me later that night. I kept tossing and turning, listening to the occasional sounds of the night. I imagined it was the last-minute nerves that were keeping me up. I did not deal well with emotions and goodbyes.

So I got up around four in the morning and thought to myself that I probably should just slip quietly away as I didn't want to cause a fuss. I knew I wouldn't be able to properly face all the emotions and will end up getting more upset than I already was. But it turned out that I didn't have a say in it because as I opened the door carrying my little suitcase with my whole life's possessions in it, I found

Clarice standing right outside as if she knew I was planning on sneaking out on her. She walked to the main road with me, where we shared a taxi to Georgetown. As we reached the place, I found out that Clarice had a friend who resided there and who was willing to drive me to the airport.

I boarded the plane and watched out of the window as the plane taxied down the runway. Then it took off and disappeared into the clouds. As Guyana disappeared out of sight, tears rolled slowly down my cheeks. I was finally leaving this place that had brought me so much unhappiness and pain, but there was also a bittersweet feeling that I was leaving something important behind. All my memories of that place were stained, but I was feeling a sense of loss. Human emotions are strange, aren't they? I was immensely glad that I was indeed finally leaving, but there was that small part of me that was regretting the decision. I told myself that it was understandable and that, of course, after living my entire life there, I would feel a bit sad.

After a long flight, I finally arrived at Lester Bird International Airport, where I was met by SSGT White, who had come to pick me up and take me to Longfords Police Training School.

They gave me supper, and I hit the sack immediately after gobbling down the food. The travelling had taken a toll on me, and I was jetlagged and exhausted.

The next morning all the recruits from Course # 29 meet and were put into groups. There were men from Barbados, Dominica, St Vincent, Grenada, St Kitts, and of course, Guyana.

My first impressions of my new home were nothing short of awestriking. Everything looked new and wonderful, and I couldn't wait to have a proper look around. The barracks rooms, too, were nothing like the ones I had back in Guyana. These had single beds with a kitchen and a mess room situated on the ground floor to the side. There were also classrooms and a drill square in the front, which was the place for our blood, sweat, and tears.

There was only one way in and one way out of Longfords Training School for the traffic, but there was a shortcut on foot to the nearby village of Cedar Grove.

From the inside of the barracks, you could see the blue Caribbean Sea with its white sands. The view was magnificent, and I felt enchanted every time I looked at it. There were big fancy hotels all around with banana boats, bars and restaurants. This was a whole new world for me. I felt like I could actually be happy here. I breathed in the fresh air of the sea and smiled to myself.

Not everything, however, was perfect. Antigua was a very hot island, and by midday, it was at its hottest. The instructors made proper use of this time to punish the recruits who were in need of it. A failed inspection for having dirty boots or an unmade bed in that heat was a punishment that I most certainly strived to avoid. Sometimes you would be given a loaded rifle and made to hold it above your head and run around the yard, making sure that you don't lower it or drop it. It could get cruel and brutal, but I understood that it was the requirement. As police officers, we needed to learn to survive in the worst of situations, and it would be better if we were prepared for everything our job threw at us.

In order to have liberty or time off at the weekends, you were required to pass all the inspections every day.

Friday night was the night for us all to go out to St Johns, where there would be BBQs. The air would be lit up with the smells of roasted chicken and corn. There were also late-night reggae parties. This was the night of the week that I most looked forward to. It was the time when I could relax and just live.

There were cinemas and several fairgrounds too but the most famous place to be at on a Saturday night was Miller's, located by the sea. They would watch live reggae bands on Sunday nights at Shirley Heights as the sun was setting. It was beautiful scenery. The whole environment was dazzling. Listening to the background reggae music while watching the setting sun was something I could not dream of while living in Guyana.

My police buddies and I would dress up in the latest fashion trends and hit the road. We would pull together and hire a car back in the early days before we had our own car. We would then take turns driving every weekend to make it fair. It was a great time to bond with my mates and just sit back and relax.

People would come across from other islands just to party with the young police officers. They loved it because it meant that they could go anywhere behind the stage to the VIP Lounge. Because we were officers of the law, no one would challenge us, and the people we took with us never had to join the long queue at nightclubs. It was an unfair and unethical use of our power, but we were young men in training who had mostly come from places that did not give us the chance to allow ourselves such freedom. When the opportunity did fall in our laps, we grabbed it.

There was a lot to cram into such a short weekend from Friday night till midnight Sunday. It was like a stampede on a Friday night because everyone was incredibly excited to finally get out after a long and hectic week. Especially for us, training was heavy work, both mentally and physically. The time we got on the weekends was invaluable, and there was too much fun to be had.

Chapter 18: The Move To England

After I had trained and served as a police officer, I once again started to feel restless because I wanted more from life, and this job and this place were failing in doing that. My purpose did not feel fulfilled, so I planned to leave and try my luck in England.

I said my goodbyes to all my new friends and made the brave move to England. Once I arrived there, I soon felt at home. I had got a job and a new home and felt, at last, this was where I belonged. It was initially a challenging move, but my move from Guyana told me that there was nothing I could not endure.

I got a job with the Derby City Council through an agency. It was a well-reputed place which would help my experience if I managed to get a job there. I told myself that I would try my best. So I was out to impress. I decided that in order to prove my worth, I needed to show people I was willing to work hard and did not eschew earning my keep. I went to the workplace early and set to work cleaning the mess room and the toilets. I made sure that the vans were all clean and ready for the day's work. All this was done before the working day actually began.

This was something that no one else had ever done. The manager clocked me doing this several times and praised me for my efforts.

One day, I was called into the Manager's Office and was asked if I would like to take the job on a permanent basis. I had done it. My efforts and hard work to gain a permanent position had been fruitful.

I was delighted. I told him, "I would love to!" with great excitement. "There would be nothing more I'd love to do," I added, gleeful at my turn of luck in the new foreign land.

So the manager told me to go to the agency and tell them that I had found full-time work and will not be needing them anymore. "Don't worry," said the manager to me, "I will still pay you for the week, and you can start for me on Monday." I felt indebted to him, in all honesty. "Have you got parking for a van at home Michael?' asked my new manager. "Yes, I do, Sir," I replied. "That's great! He exclaimed. "Because from Monday, you will have your own van."

As I left my new office and went outside, I just couldn't control myself much longer. I felt like I would burst with gratitude and excitement. I yelled, "YES! YES!" as I punched the air and jumped up and down like a child whose wishes had come true.

The first few weeks were very trying for me. My supervisor was a middle-aged white man who had it in for me right from the beginning. It started with little things, like name-calling, etc.

One day, I was backing the works van into the shed. It was a very tight squeeze with only a foot on each side for clearance. Charlie, the supervisor, began clapping after I had parked the van, a burst of mocking laughter escaping him. He shouted, "YOU LOT HAVE COME A LONG WAY."

I turned to him and asked, "I beg your pardon?" Charlie replied, "You know, from swinging in the trees and beating your chests. Look at you now. You can drive and talk." He was roaring with laughter.

Charlie turned away. I had to bite my lip in order to keep quiet. I kept thinking about how much I needed the job, which helped me stop myself from reacting. After all, I was on probation. Charlie continued to have digs at me for the next few weeks, trying his best to provoke me.

One day, a few of the guys were off sick, so the Manager asked Charlie if he and I could go down to Stockbrook Street, prune the bushes and shrubs. "Yes, no problem," said Charlie. So we loaded the van up with all the tools and drove off. I started to unload the van when we arrived there, and as soon as that was done, Charlie told me to start the van as he had to go somewhere and drove off in the van before I could say anything. My flask and lunch were still in the van, but before I could protest or do anything, he was gone.

The only thing I could do was make a start on the cutting and trimming without him. I was cutting back the hedge when I heard a knock on the window, so I walked over and saw a pale-looking woman with silver hair, a kind face, and a very proper Derby accent.

"Fancy a cuppa lad?" She asked me in her comical thick accent. "Oh yes, please," I replied, slightly content to see a friendly-looking face. "You are doing a grand job there, lad." she chirped before walking off to make the drink. After drinking the much-needed cup of tea, I placed the cup on the windowsill and carried on with work, my spirits somewhat raised.

By the time Charlie returned, I had finished all the jobs that were assigned to us. I was cold and hungry and told Charlie that I was going to have my dinner and a hot drink. But Charlie wasn't having any of it. He rolled the window of the van down and screamed at me. "NO FUCKING WAY. LOAD THE VAN UP FIRST." I was done with his attitude and refused. I told him I needed to get warm and have something to eat.

He wasn't having any of it. He barked at me again. "NO WAY." I was exhausted after all the labour and did not have it in me to argue with him any further. Apart from that, he could easily have me fired, and I could not afford that. I decided to let it go. "Have it your way," I sighed and sat on the wall outside St Luke's Church, leaning on the hoe that I had used to do the shrubs. At this, Charlie jumped out of the van and stormed over to where I leaned and bellowed, "LOAD THE FUCKING VAN UP, YOU BLACK BASTARD." I ignored him again, but apparently, that was not the reaction he wanted out of me, so Charlie placed his hand on my forehead and pushed hard. "YOU THINK JUST BECAUSE YOU'RE A BIG CUNT IM SCARED OF YOU?" He yelled again. "I don't want you to be scared of me," I answered him in a soft low voice at which Charlie pushed me again.

My patience was running out, and I told myself that I would not be responsible for any action that I took against the bastard. I tried to avoid conflict again and tried to warn him in a low hissing sound, my voice betraying the anger I felt inside my bones. "I wouldn't do that again if I were you." But Charlie pushed and pushed me again. I gave him my final warning, "I won't be responsible for my actions if you continue to push me." But Charlie did continue. I took one step backwards and swung the hoe at the back of Charlie's legs, and he fell down hard. But he turned out to be a stickler for pushing my buttons and getting beaten up because that was not an isolated incident.

I decided that I could not continue working in his presence as he had taken the joy out of my life and made working seem more like a punishment. I had already suffered enough abuse in my life, and I did not have the stomach for more. I reported him to the Manager who called Charlie in his office and told him that he was moving him to a different site. Nothing more was said, and peace was restored in my life.

Chapter 19: Meeting Angela In 2015

After I had met and married a woman in Derby who already had two small children and went on to have another child with me, my relationship with her started to show cracks. It was not a happy marriage from the beginning, so I should not have been surprised.

After some years, I had split up with my now ex-wife and went through all the heartbreak and devastation that a breakup causes. I am not proud to say that those were some of the worst days of my life.

I had lost everything that mattered to me, my family, and my home. I just didn't know where to turn. Everywhere I went, I could only see darkness and no way out of that foreign maze.

I had yet again trusted someone only to be betrayed, so I decided that I was going to build myself a wall around my heart, and I was going to build it high and let no one in again.

Because of that wall, I drifted in and out of relationships with little or no feelings at all.

I spent my nights in bars seven days a week. Everyone around the town knew me; all the doormen, all the bar staff, and all the regulars in the pubs.

I wasn't eating, just drinking my life away, but I still managed to go to work every day. All my workmates noticed my weight loss and tried to tell me, but I wasn't having any of it.

I didn't like this life, but I would rather be like this than go through the heartache and misery ever again. My strategy to never let anyone in my life close enough to hurt me was working, but I was losing myself in that process.

I had a lot of different spirits in my own bar, which I had collected from all around the world. From the minute I finished work, I would go home and hit the bottle, drink myself into oblivion. I would fall asleep wherever I fell. Sometimes I would find myself in my back garden. My life had no meaning at the moment, and I was merely living for the sake of it.

I had to sell the house, so when it was sold subject to contract, I had to start looking somewhere else to live, but because of bad credit, this made it very difficult. I was struggling to find somewhere as no one would touch me with my credit history.

It was only by chance that I bumped into an old friend. I asked her if she knew any cheap place I could rent. I explained how things had gone, how desperate I was, and that circumstances called that I move out quickly.

After only a few days, I got a call from my friend Lorraine. She told me she could help me. She had spoken to her family and decided that she would rent out her small back bedroom to me until I got back on my feet.

I couldn't believe it. I was overjoyed and grateful to her. After Lorraine had looked around to check out what price to charge me, a date was set for me to move in.

I asked my good friend Lance if he could help me move in, and of course, Lance was only happy to help his mate.

Once I was settled in, Lorraine sat me down and set out the rules: no women, no family were allowed in, and no friends were allowed in either.

I sat there and thought to myself that it was a bit harsh but, well, beggars cannot be choosers. After work, I always went straight to bed for a couple of hours. As social life in the house was not possible for me.

When I was on the night shift or on days off, I would shower, get ready, and hit the town, but Lorraine didn't like this very much. She would nag me not just about going out but about my hair in the bath, too, for bits of my hair were found on the landing.

I remember one day when I had used the dryer and the washing machine, Lorraine shouted at me in a very thick

Jamaican accent, "A WAH DIS?" I went into the kitchen to see what all the fuss was about; she was standing there, hands on both hips, looking at the dryer. "What's up? I asked her.

"DIS, MAN," she grimaced, pointing to the dryer, which had a small bit of fluff in it. "It's from your clothes. You must clean it out when ya finished."

Needless to say, that was the last time I used the washer or dryer. I had never lived with anyone like her before. She had told me to treat the house like my own, to watch the TV when I wanted to, and watch my sports programmes when I wanted to. So one day, while Lorraine was out, I sat down to watch a car show, and when I had finished it, I turned off the TV with the remote and went back to my room. It was a completely normal thing to do, I had guessed.

However, when Lorraine got home she wasn't happy with the way I had turned off the TV, so she gave me a lesson on how to turn the TV off. I was a bit gobsmacked by all this. I did not realize there were different ways of turning the TV off.

But it wasn't all bad living there. We actually had some long, meaningful conversations and laughed a lot too.

I continued to go into town for my own sense of freedom and to be around other people. Not necessarily to interact with them, but just to have a drink. I would sometimes get drunk and finish the evening with my usual chicken and chips from Mamma Janes, my favorite shop in Derby.

One Friday night, I was out in the local bar called THE TIGER BAR. I loved it in there. I knew the DJ and the bar staff, some of the regulars as well. The music was great too. The DJ played some good tunes. It was, all in all, a good way of letting off some steam and relax after a hard day's work.

I bought two bottled beers and gave one to the DJ, after which I went and stood in my usual spot and sipped my beer, watching people come in and go out, watching as they had fun on the dance floor.

I was doing this that day, too, my routine unchanged, when I noticed a group of ladies walk into the bar. They went and ordered their drinks, and in no time at all, they were on the dance floor dancing around, having a great time. Then there she was, blonde and beautiful, sexy and most definitely the heart and soul of the party.

At the same time, there was an older gent dancing by himself who was wearing a flat cap, and the blonde took his cap off him and put it on her own head, dancing around the floor with him.

That was when my eyes met hers for the first time. She had the biggest and brightest eyes I had ever seen. They shone like two of the brightest stars in the galaxy. After returning the cap to the old gent, she danced her way over to me. "Hi," she chirped. "Do you want to come and dance?" But me being me, stone cold in my demeanor, replied, "Nah, I am alright." She insisted, but I stood my ground and once again told her it was okay. My defiance was unmoved.

It was then that I noticed she was wearing a wedding ring. Bitter memories resurfaced inside me, and I told her to get away from me and back home to her husband. She just looked at me with her sad eyes and said to me, in a melancholic voice said that she was moving out of the house and in with her daughter and husband and their three boys. She tried to tell me how unhappy she was. She told me about her husband and their three boys and that it was not going to work out with her husband. I shook my head, and a bitter laugh escaped me. "Yeah, it always is. Now fuck off". "Oh," she looked hurt but did not say anything else and returned back to her friends.

For the next hour, she stayed with her friends but kept on looking over at me, so I decided to drink up and move on to the next pub.

My next stop was a pub called THE JORROCKS. Then I went to SADDIES, THE SUNLOUNGE, THE WHITE HEART, and then settled in the METRO BAR. My escapades finally ended there.

I said my hellos to the bar staff and DJ Dave. I ordered my drink, looked around through the crowds, and there she was again, only this time, shall we say, she was a bit braver because by now she had had a few drinks. She approached me once again.

"Hello again," she began, "What's your name?" "I'm Michael," I drawled, feigning boredom.

"Well, hello, Michael, I'm Angie." At that, she took me by the hand and introduced me to her friends before I could protest or say another word.

"Are you on Facebook?" was the next question. I said I was.

"So add me then." "I will."

"No, do it now." She was having none of my excuses. My clipped responses did not seem to bother her, so I sighed and surrendered.

I took my phone out, and she watched me add her. After that, she wrote down her number on a beer mat. Despite my hard exterior and previous rude comments, I could not help but smile at her.

"Right, come on then," she said. We are going for a dance."

Once again, before I could say no, I was being pulled against my will and onto the dance floor.

I had to admit that she was fun, and I did enjoy myself. We even had a kiss and what we call dry humping on the dance floor. It was hilarious, and I was laughing out loud.

I knew the doorman there, and he was watching me with a big smile on his face. At this point, Angie was quite drunk and tried to pull me into the ladies' toilet with her. My mate Steve told me to go in and that he will watch the door for me. No way was I going to the toilet with her. I stepped my foot down, and straight-up refused. So Angie went to the loo on her own. When she returned, she was all over me, and her friends were trying to make her leave me alone, for they were scared that someone who knew her would tell on her. I believed she had forgotten she was married. But from what she had admitted to me, it was about to end any time soon anyway. Still, adultery couldn't be seen in a positive light by anyone anywhere, that too so publicly.

When it was time to go, Angie thought that she would have one last go at making her move on me and pulled me down the Primark loading bay. But the lights came on, and that sealed the end of her advances. Her friends took her to get her some sobering kebab, and presumably, she went home.

I thought that would be my final meeting with her, but the very next day, I got a message from her on Facebook. I had got her number, but I hadn't given her mine for the simple reason that I just wasn't looking to take this any further than it already had. My past experiences were sounding an alarm in my head, and I was feeling vulnerable again.

Another relationship was the last thing on my mind. However, we did continue to talk through Facebook Messenger for a couple of days. Despite maintaining the fact that I was careful.

I then went on a planned road trip for three weeks. Angie was upset with me because I hadn't told her that I had gone, but we chatted the time I was away.

It was when I was away that she left her husband and moved in with her daughter. I had been back from my trip for nearly three weeks before we chatted again, and from there, we arranged to meet for the first time at the local pub called MR G DRUDIS. I arrived first so sat at the nearest table, waiting for her.

Angie walked in looking phenomenal. Hair all done, makeup on, and to top all that, she wore a bewitching smile. She walked over to me and sat down with poise. We chatted all night long. It turned out to be a magical evening.

When it was time to go, I asked her if she would like to go into town for another drink. Of course, she was ready for that additional drink, so that was what we did. We both enjoyed it very much and chatted some more. Then we danced a little, and I walked her home.

I did meet her up now and again for drinks and went for walks around the local park. When Angie was out with the girls, she would arrange to meet up with me at some point in the evening.

One of these evenings, she was out with her daughter Sarah and some mates. She was sitting outside the pub all by herself, having a smoke when I turned the corner and saw her. I walked over to her, gave her a peck, and greeted her with a sweet "hi". That was when Sarah came out. We were introduced to each other by Angie and got along splendidly from the start. Then we went out to have fun and enjoyed the evening.

I continued to see Angie, and we decided it would be nice if we could get away for a long weekend somewhere. It was decided that we would book a hotel in Birmingham. A few weeks later, I picked her up from Sarah's house, and off we went.

There was no awkwardness between us in the car. In fact, we chatted non-stop, and soon enough, we were in

Birmingham. We booked in, had a shower, and made love for the first time. It felt heavenly. So good, in fact, that we did it again before going out to see the nightlife.

It was a wonderful weekend, but like everything else, it had to come to an end. On the way home, we were both a bit quiet. I suppose we were a little sad it had to end and I had to return back to work. Neither of us said it, but both of us wanted to stay there forever. Make continuous love, forget ourselves, and not think about the rest of the world.

Our relationship was growing into something more. I tried my hardest not to fall for her, but it was almost impossible not to. I thought about her every day, and I knew she was falling for me deeply despite neither of us wanting a serious relationship, but we just couldn't help it. Now that I think of it, I believe it was inevitable, and fighting our strong feelings would have been fruitless.

Sometime after, Angie was offered a flat by the council. It was only a one-bedroom place - a bit small - but she took it as it was near Sarah's place. In fact, it was within walking distance, and she would finally be moving out of her daughter's place and stand on her ground, be independent.

Sarah had helped Angie move into the flat, and when I finished work, I went around to see her. I must say I was very surprised to see that she was already unpacked. She had already put up pictures on the wall, although she didn't have many but to her credit, she had made it very cosy.

I decided to take her out to celebrate her new home. We had another lovely night out, and we spent the first night in her own place together. I thought it was rather romantic.

It wasn't long before I was spending more and more time there, only going back to Lorraine's maybe one or two nights a week.

We decided to book a holiday to Italy for ten days. This trip did something to our relationship, and we connected on a deeper, more spiritual level. It really showed me that it had been a brilliant idea to come away together because it cemented the relationship that I was trying to avoid so hard. I realized that I had failed in my endeavors to stay away from love.

I was never meant to fall in love, but I could feel that I was. My being was screaming at me, telling me that I had fallen head over heels for her. But I didn't want to tell her that. Admitting I loved her meant that I was putting myself in a vulnerable situation once again. It meant for me that my relationship with her was real and held consequences. It did not matter that she had already told me she was in love with me. My previous relationship had scarred me beyond doubt, and despite Angie being my perfect match, I wanted to pull away from her.

When we returned from Italy, I again stayed with her at her flat. However, I had to go home at some point as I was still paying rent to Lorraine. Angie used to get upset when I went because then she was on her own for quite a long time. Though she did go up to see Sarah for girl's nights, or Sarah would come to the flat for drinks. Some of her friends would visit her as well at times. But the fact that I could not spend all my time with her used to bum her out a lot.

Our first Christmas was spent at the flat. Angie put up the tree, and then we went out for food shopping. Sarah had invited us on Boxing Day to hers, and the time that we had, there was incredible. My heart warms still when I think about it.

Angie's son Martin came to visit us with his girlfriend Natalie, which was always nice. Even my daughters came to see us at the flat since they were not allowed to visit me at Lorraine's house.

We soon started to talk about moving in together, but I had to tell Angie something that I hadn't told her yet. One morning before going to work, I kissed her goodbye, bent down, and whispered "I love you" in her ear. She looked at me and her eyes filled with tears. She couldn't speak, and I went off to work with a smile on my face.

After that, a day has not passed without us saying that we love each other.

We made the resolution to move in together, but because the flat was almost minuscule, we decided it would be better if we looked for something bigger.

Angie got to the point where she didn't like going out because of seeing her ex around town, and I was not comfortable either, just in case I saw my ex. Both of us had terrible unhappy memories attached to those people, and we did not want their presence tarnishing our newfound happiness. We had thought long and hard about moving away from Derby, so that is what we did.

We did upset family and friends by doing so, but we were offered a massive bungalow in Staffordshire. It was beautiful and had everything we needed, from a very big garage for my American car – a 1966 Impala - to a lovely big garden at the back and a garden at the front. It was perfect and more than what I could have dreamed for.

After being there for over a year, the landlord sold the bungalow without telling us. It came as an unfortunate shock when we were informed that we only had three months to find a new place before the new owners moved in.

We had made friends with the couple up the road, Hazel and Charlie. They made our moving out easier and were never out of comforting words. Angie was more upset than I was because I had thought something like this would happen. In my heart, I always knew that it was too good to be true, and I had learnt from life experience not to expect anything more. Even though I was ecstatic living with Angie, I had never fully let go of my fears and pessimism. But it turned out the gods were looking after us and had never abandoned me, although I did not once expect anything great from my life. We found ourselves in another one-bedroom bungalow which we loved, and soon made it our home, putting our own spin on it. Since then, we have been calling it our happy place. It has a lovely big garden at the front and an even bigger one at the back. I could not believe it at first, but our move turned out to be for the better.

We organized parties after parties for our loved ones and had a great time when all our friends and family members came over to participate in our good times. We also joined the local club at our walking distance and made new friends, and socialised with people from different walks of life.

Then in March 019, Angie got what she had wished for. Yes, her divorce papers arrived in the post, and believe me when I say that they were signed, sealed, and sent back the same day. We had spoken about getting married after Angie proposed to me via text the year before, but she said she did it through a text message because she thought I'd say no, and it would be less embarrassing. But I didn't say no. In fact, we went straight to the registrar to set the date.

August 31st, 2019, at 4:30 pm, was the happiest day of my life. We were married, and the whole day was downright perfect. Everyone turned up with the help of Hazel and our well-wishers. Martin gave his mum away, and my best friend Janson was my best man. We used the Impala as the wedding car with my Friend Trevor driving it. I could not believe I was capable of such warmth and happiness. My heart was swooning looking at my dazzling new bride.

My little granddaughters were flower girls. Seeing my daughters and granddaughters at my wedding was the icing on the cake. I can easily say nothing will ever come close to my wedding day. It has a special place in my heart.

We now live a happy and contented life together, and not a day passes without us reminding each other of the love we have in our hearts for one another. God willing, we will continue to live a happy and healthy life till we are old and grey.